ANTI-SEMITISM

KETER BOOKS

This book is compiled from material originally published in the *Encyclopaedia Judaica*

Copyright © 1974, Keter Publishing House Jerusalem Ltd.
P.O. Box 7145, Jerusalem, Israel

Cat. No. 25068
ISBN 0 7065 1327 4

Printed in Israel

CONTENTS

CHRONOLOGY

Additional information on the Holocaust (the destruction of European Jewry 1933–45) will be found in the volume in this series entitled *Holocaust*.

CONTRIBUTORS

Prof Yizhak Heinemann (deceased): Philosopher and scholar of Jewish Hellenism, Jerusalem

Prof. Joshua Gutmann (deceased): Emeritus Associate Professor of Jewish History and Jewish Hellenism, the Hebrew University of Jerusalem

Dr. Leon Poliakov: Maître de Recherches, Centre National de la Recherche Scientifique, Paris

Paul Weissman: Jerusalem

Dr. Arthur Hertzberg, Rabbi: Associate Adjunct Professor of History, Columbia University, New York

Dr. Yehoshafat Harkabi: Major General (Res.), Israel Defense Forces: Senior Lecturer in International Relations and Middle Eastern Studies, the Hebrew University of Jerusalem

Dr. Binyamin Eliav: Editor and former official, Ministry for Foreign Affairs, Jerusalem

Prof. Haim Hillel Ben-Sasson: Professor of Jewish History, the Hebrew University of Jerusalem

Prof. Yehuda Slutsky: Professor of History of the Israel Labor Movement, Tel Aviv University

Dr. Bernhard Blumenkranz: Maître de Recherches, Centre National de la Recherche Scientifique, Paris

B. Mordechai Ansbacher: Historian, Jerusalem

Prof. Cecil Roth (deceased): Reader Emeritus in Jewish Studies, the University of Oxford: Editor in Chief of the *Encyclopaedia Judaica*, Jerusalem

Yvonne Glikson: Editor, *Encyclopaedia Judaica*, Jerusalem

David Corcos: Editor, *Encyclopaedia Judaica*, Jerusalem

Prof. Jacob Toury: Associate Professor of Jewish History, Tel Aviv University

Dr. Pavel Korzec: Research Associate of the Centre National de la Recherche Scientifique, Paris

Dr. Shaoul Langnas: Jewish Agency, Tel Aviv

Dr. Theodor Lavi: Historian, Yad Vashem, Jerusalem

Dr. Baruch Yaron: Librarian, the Hebrew University of Jerusalem

Dr. William Korey: Director of the B'nai B'rith United Nations Office, New York

Ernest Hearst: Editor, Wiener Library, London

Dr. Moshé Catane: Senior Lecturer in French Civilization and Literature, Bar Ilan University, Ramat Gan; Librarian, the Jewish National and University Library, Jerusalem

Chasia Turtel: Researcher in Jewish History, Jerusalem

Dr. Avigdor Dagan: Ambassador and author, Ministry for Foreign Affairs, Jerusalem

Dr. Jonathan Frankel: Senior Lecturer in Russian Studies and Contemporary Jewish Studies, the Hebrew University of Jerusalem

1 ANTI-SEMITISM

The above term was coined in 1879, from the Greek $\dot{\alpha}\nu\tau\acute{\iota}$ = anti, and $\Sigma\eta\mu$ = Semite by the German agitator Wilhelm Marr to designate the then-current anti-Jewish campaigns in Europe. "Anti-Semitism" soon came into general use as a term denoting all forms of hostility manifested toward the Jews throughout history. It is often qualified by an adjective denoting the specific cause, nature, or rationale of a manifestation of anti-Jewish passion or action: e.g., "economic anti-Semitism," "social anti-Semitism," "racial anti-Semitism," etc.

In Antiquity. Prejudice against Jews appeared in antiquity almost exclusively in those countries which later became part of the Roman Empire. Some manifestations were noted in the Parthian Empire, which contained Babylonian Jewry, but such hatred never attained serious proportions. Josephus states it as a well-known fact that in the lands of the Babylonian exile anti-Semitism did not exist (Apion 1:71). In those countries that afterward formed part of the Roman Empire, a distinction must be drawn between Erez Israel and the Diaspora.

IN EREZ ISRAEL. Even in the days of David and Solomon the Land of Israel contained a substantial Gentile population. In Hellenistic times this was primarily concentrated in the coastal towns and in certain districts of Transjordan, but the boundaries between the Jewish and non-Jewish regions were not fixed and the seeds of friction were ever present. Of particular importance, however, was the difference in occupations between the Jews and Gentiles of those areas. The Jewish population engaged principally in   1 agriculture, particularly in small-scale farming; the non-Jewish population occupied itself primarily with commerce. The transit and sea trade was almost entirely in the hands of the inhabitants of the coastal cities, or of the Transjordanian cities situated along the routes that connected Syria, Asia Minor, and the regions of the Euphrates with the Arabian countries. The inhabitants of Erez Israel who engaged in commerce, with connections abroad, were thus mainly non-Jewish. These Gentiles were therefore in close contact with the foreign powers in the region and were confident of their support; in Erez Israel they were contemptuous of the Jewish population, whom they regarded as an isolated people that eschewed civilization and refrained from all contact with the outside world. Moreover, the non-Jews who dwelt in Erez Israel knew that the Jews looked upon that land as their divine inheritance. In the eyes of the Jews, as these Gentiles knew, their pagan religions and practices rendered them "unclean"; intermarriage with them was forbidden and, as a consequence of the dietary laws, no real social intercourse was possible.

In normal times these two segments of the population dwelt alongside each other without any undue hostility. In time of crisis, however, relations deteriorated sharply. The first serious manifestation of anti-Semitism in history was the concentrated attack on the Jewish religion in the days of Antiochus Epiphanes[1] (175–164 B.C.E.). The immediate cause was anger of the Seleucids[2] at the fact that the vast majority of Jews traditionally sided with the Ptolemies[3] against the Seleucids. Tension was exacerbated still further by the image that Hellenistic rulers such as Antiochus had of themselves. Their role was not only political; they were also to be torchbearers of the ideals of Hellenism[4] within their dominions. The seeming unfriendliness of the Jews

[1] Seleucid monarch, ruled Syria 175–164 B.C.E.
[2] Royal dynasty, ruled in Syria 312–65 B.C.E.
[3] Royal dynasty, ruled in Egypt 323–30 B.C.E.
[4] Term indicating the culture that obtained its ideas from classical Greek civilization and spread over the empire of Alexander and other countries

2

toward all Gentiles, and their hostility to every other religion, was therefore seen as an obstacle to the realization of this cultural mission. An echo of this attitude can be seen in the account of the negotiations that took place outside Jerusalem in 133 B.C.E., when John Hyrcanus[5] was compelled to yield to Antiochus Sidetes[6] after the latter had besieged the capital for a year. Antiochus Sidetes' officers counseled him to seize the opportunity to conquer the city and completely destroy the Jewish people, since the Jews were the only people in the world that refused to associate with other peoples. Pressing the point, they reminded Antiochus Sidetes of the course taken by Antiochus Epiphanes, who undertook to abrogate those laws of the Torah that he regarded as inimical to humanity. To this end, he had sacrificed a swine on the altar at Jerusalem and ordered that juices from the sacrificial flesh be sprinkled over the books containing the statutes that were directed against the Gentile world (Diodorus, *Bibliotheca,* 34:1, 1ff.).

This reiterated insistence on the alleged antipathy of the Jews to other nations is best understood against the background of the peculiar conditions and circumstances obtaining in the Hellenistic period.[7] No other nation at that time denied the gods of its neighbors; on the contrary, it recognized them, identifying them with its own deities. This pan-religiosity was used with considerable success by the Hellenistic ruling authorities to create a social bond between the various peoples in their domains. None of the peoples refrained from dining at one table with their neighbors and from partaking of the sacrifices offered to their gods, except the Jews. None of the peoples refused to send gifts to its neighbors' temples, except the Jews. None of the peoples was unequivocally hostile to intermarriage, except the Jews. They characterized it as a misanthropy, a

---

[5] Ethnarch of Judea and high priest (135–104 B.C.E.)
[6] Antiochus VII, Seleucid monarch, ruled Syria 138–128 B.C.E.
[7] The period between 4th cent. B.C.E. and 2nd cent C.E.

flagrant denial of the Hellenic principle of the unity of mankind.

As the Hasmonean[8] kingdom expanded and established its dominion over the whole land, its kings occasionally adopted a policy of political and religious oppression vis à vis the inhabitants of the pagan cities of Palestine, who had sided earlier with Antiochus Epiphanes and had joined the war of Antiochus Sidetes against the Jews. Against this background, libels began to circulate, denying that the Jews had any right to remain in the land. Underlying these libels were Egyptian legends concerning shepherd kings who had once ruled over Egypt and oppressed its people but who had subsequently been expelled. There were also stories about a leprous or unclean people who had been banished from Egypt so that the land and its temples, which they had defiled, might be purified. These legends were now related to the biblical tale of the Exodus; the composite version was that the Jews had been expelled from Egypt because of their uncleanliness and had continued to separate themselves from the other nations in Erez Israel. If such was their origin and the reason for their present habits, they had no legitimate claims on this or any other land.

Descriptions of the Jews as homeless wanderers are found in the allegations of Antiochus Sidetes' officers, who regarded their nomadic status as justification for destroying them. The general motif, however, is undoubtedly much older, having been employed by non-Jews to counter the Jewish claim that Erez Israel was the inheritance of the Lord and that idolaters had no share in it. However, if in the period preceding the Hasmonean conquests this Jewish conception of Erez Israel made little practical difference to its non-Jewish inhabitants, in the Hasmonean epoch it became the justification for eradicating idolatry from the land, and not idolatry alone. The sins of the Canaanites, as they are enumerated in the Wisdom of Solomon (12: 3ff.),

---

[8] A priestly family and dynasty, who headed the rebellion against the Seleucid kingdom and established an autonomous Jewish State (the 2nd and 1st centuries B.C.E.)

an apocryphal book composed in this period, were depicted as so offensive to the Holy Land that their perpetrators would have to be cast out if they did not mend their ways and conduct themselves in a manner compatible with the sanctity of Ereẓ Israel. The reaction of Israel's enemies to such an outlook is not difficult to fathom.

With the consolidation of Roman rule in Palestine there was apparently little reason for the Jews of Palestine to obstruct the policy pursued by Rome on its eastern borders. Even the attempts at such obstruction in the time of Antiochus II [9] (e.g., his approach to the Parthians), and by the war party during the war which led to the destruction of the Second Temple, constituted no great danger to Rome. Any anti-Semitism which then was associated with Roman foreign policy was not caused by militancy or even by revolt on the part of Palestinian Jewry. Even in the relations between the Jewish and non-Jewish settlements in Palestine, Rome created a kind of equilibrium, and clashes on any large scale between the two sides ceased completely. Fresh fuel for anti-Semitic excesses, however, was provided by emperor-worship, which had begun to assume the form of a permanent political institution in all the countries of the Roman Empire from the time of Augustus onward. From the views of contemporaries to this worship, it appears not to have been regarded as an act of religious homage to the emperor but as an expression of loyalty to the state, which was itself endowed with religious sanctity. The refusal by the Jews to accept the imperial cult in any form was thus equated in the minds of many Romans with a refusal to recognize the authority of the state, and as a result, the belief gradually began to take hold in the pagan world that the Jews had no respect for whatever was held in esteem by the rest of humanity. There was one dangerous incident when the Jews were ordered by Caligula [10] to erect and worship an image of the emperor in Jerusalem, but his assassination spared the Jews of Palestine and other parts of

[9] Seleucid monarch, ruled Syria 261–246 B.C.E.
[10] Roman emperor 37–41 C.E.

the Roman Empire a bitter conflict with the imperial authorities.

IN THE DIASPORA. The Jews of the Roman Empire (unlike their later-day descendants in the late Middle Ages) were not, as a rule, restricted in regard to place of residence; according to the testimony of reliable sources, there was no part of the empire where Jews were not to be found. The Jews formed up to 10–12%, approximately, of the population of the empire, and since an appreciable portion of the Jews in the Diaspora were found in the cities, it follows that they played an important role in the economic life of the countries in which they lived (Jos., Ant., 14:115). It would also seem that the Jews were as unrestricted in their choice of occupation as they were in their choice of residence. In regard to their legal position, no discrimination was made between them and the other citizens of the empire, the extent of their rights being dependent, as a rule, on the class to which they belonged. In some cases Jews even received favored treatment in deference to their religious needs. The observance of the Sabbath and fulfillment of other religious precepts led them to seek exemptions from certain civic obligations which were imposed upon the rest of the populace. According to Josephus[11] (Ant., 14:187, 190ff.), the prerogatives granted the Jews were protected by special decrees of the kings of Persia and Macedonia, and even the Roman rulers honored them, without thereby arousing popular resentment.

About the first century B.C.E., however, several factors brought about a radical change. In Egypt, particularly in Alexandria, strong opposition to Roman rule became manifest, for many reasons. The upper strata of Alexandrian Egyptians had particular cause for complaint. They had directed the country's policies during the reign of the Ptolemies but they were now, under Rome, out of power. They were thus reduced to a level no higher than that of the

[11] Jewish historian (c. 38-after 100 C.E.)

Jews, who were now competing with the former ruling class for Roman favor. Relations inevitably deteriorated.

Illuminating in this respect are the orders issued by the emperor Claudius soon after the restoration of quiet in Alexandria, following the turbulence resulting from the riots organized by the Greeks against the Jewish settlement there. In his injunction to the citizens of Alexandria and the Syrian cities (Jos., Ant., 19:279ff.) Claudius fully confirms the original privileges granted to the Jews to allow them to keep the precepts of the Torah without let or hindrance. However, in his edict to all the countries of the empire, in which Claudius addresses himself to the Jews as well, after reaffirming their right to observe the commandments of the Torah, he declares: "I enjoin upon them also by these presents to avail themselves of this kindness in a more reasonable spirit, and not to set at nought the beliefs about the gods held by other peoples, but to keep their own laws" (Ant., 19:286ff., especially 290). Claudius, in an edict to the Alexandrians which has been preserved in a papyrus (published by Idris Bell), is even more explicit. In it, after stating that the Jews are completely at liberty to observe the injunctions of the Torah, Claudius warns that if they will not content themselves with the rights accorded them, he will employ against them all such means as should be used against people who spread "a general plague throughout the world." This expression would seem to derive from the canard then current in quarters hostile to the Jews that they were a danger to the Gentile world.

Despite the friction between Judaism and the centers of Hellenistic-Roman culture in Egypt, Syria, and in other cities of the Roman Empire adverse to the Jews, no change was made in the Roman legal code. However, Judaism and the Jews were increasingly described as flouting not only the law, but all of human society, among a number of groups in which the writers and intellectuals of Hellenic-Roman society were prominent. Though the elements of such characterizations had all already appeared during the struggle between the Hasmonean kings and their adversaries in Palestine, in the first century C.E. they were arranged into a kind of connected rationale of anti-Jewishness.

In common with the courtiers of Antiochus Sidetes two centuries earlier, many Greek authors of the first century C.E. portrayed the Jewish people as the descendants of a mob of lepers, a contaminated rabble, whom the Egyptians had cast out to purge themselves of their defilement and who had continued to pursue in Judea, their adopted home, the pattern that accorded with their degenerate and outcast state. Thus, as unclean people who had been afflicted with leprosy, they shunned the flesh of swine, this creature being more prone than others to contract this disease. The observance of the Sabbath and the worship of God by the Jews in general were interpreted in a similar vein. No stranger was permitted to approach the Temple in Jerusalem because human beings were sacrificed there. A number of writers of the first century C.E. attempted to portray Jewish life in this manner, the most prominent among them being Chaeremon, Nero's teacher; Lysimachus of Alexandria, the head of the library at Alexandria; and Apion,[12] who surpassed all the others in the crudeness of his fabrications. The destruction of the Second Temple added fuel to the fire. In the period immediately preceding this event, visions of the redemption of the world from the Roman yoke in a form closely corresponding to that of Jewish eschatology began to spread within sections of pagan society. The attraction of the idea of redemption, with its attendant liberation from the ruling power, was a great boon to the propagation of the message of Judaism, the recognition of the unity of God being inextricably interwoven with the redemptive vision. The destruction of the Temple at this juncture produced a sharp counterreaction to this ferment, many of the Jewish adversaries seizing upon it and upon the catastrophe that befell Judea and the

8 [12] Greek anti-Jewish propagandist in Alexandria (1st cent. C.E.)

Jewish colonies in Alexandria, Antioch, and Cyrene as evidence that the Jews were hated by God and had received their due punishment at His hands. According to a story from an anti-Semitic source (Philostratus, *Vita Apollonii,* 6:29), when representatives of the peoples living in proximity to Judea came and presented to Titus a wreath of victory for his destruction of Jerusalem, he declined to accept it, saying that he had only lent a hand to God, who had revealed his wrath against the Jews. Of what worth was a doctrine of world redemption propagated by a nation forsaken by its god?

The same period saw a deterioration in the attitude of a number of the representatives of the Roman aristocracy toward Jews and Judaism. The factors responsible for this change stemmed, on the one hand, from the conditions prevailing in Rome and among its ruling classes, and, on the other, from the continuing influence, even after the year 70, exerted by Judaism upon some sections of Roman society. Emperors of the type of Nero and Domitian snuffed out the last glimmer of freedom. Sycophancy and subservience dominated the atmosphere. As they dreamt of a purer past which ought to be restored, many Roman intellectuals felt hampered by the multiplicity of foreign cults in imperial Rome and by the powerful influence of Judaism, which appeared to them as subversive of the entire life pattern of Rome. The Jewish colony in Rome had already felt the barbs of a number of Roman writers (e.g., Horace and Martial), but the first Roman authors to deal with the Jews did not rise to unusual heights of invective. Even Cicero, the first writer to discuss the Jews seriously (in his speech on behalf of Lucius Valerius Flaccus, the proconsul of Asia Minor, in 62 B.C.E., he attacked the Jews of Palestine and the Diaspora, and, in particular, those of Rome), did not carry his criticism of the Jews beyond the bounds customary among the pleaders in Rome who tried to discredit a litigant in the interests of their client. It may be well to point out here that Cicero, in attacking the Gauls in defense of one of his clients, leveled such grave charges 9 against them and their religion that, by comparison, the accusations he made against the Jews were not unduly severe (cf. the fragments of Cicero's speech *Pro Pontio*).

The end of the first century C.E. witnessed a radical change. Those who saw Rome's salvation in the resuscitation of civic liberty, in the revival of the Roman attribute of *virtus,* and in the renewal of the ancient Roman ideals of heroism and justice, pointed to the danger inherent in the Jewish attempt to swamp the lower and middle classes with new ideas. They sought to rally the public to their standard by declaring the struggle against the propagators of such ideas a life and death necessity. One of the most capable and outspoken of these agitators was Cornelius Tacitus. He cited all the libelous fabrications against Jews to be culled from Greek anti-Semitic literature. His presentation of the subject as an inquiry into the various accounts of the Jews and their doctrines to the end of discovering that most consonant with historic reality, is but a futile attempt to mask his single, overriding purpose, to prove the Jews a mere rabble, hateful to the gods and men alike, and capable of gaining adherents for their degenerate cause only in a Rome that had become a breeding ground for all that was vile and abhorrent (Tacitus, *Historiae,* 5:1–13; cf. also his *Annales,* 15:44).

Juvenal followed closely in the footsteps of Tacitus. In one of his poems he portrayed a convert to Judaism as estranged from Roman society and from the members of his family, as unprepared to guide a person who has lost his way if he is not an observer of the Law of Moses, and as unwilling to give a thirsty man a drink if he is uncircumcised (Juvenal, *Saturae,* 14:96ff.). General Roman policy toward the Jews was not greatly affected by the diatribes of writers such as Tacitus or Juvenal. It is not inconceivable, however, that the emperor Hadrian's anti-Jewish policy, which represented only a brief episode in the history of Roman legislation in regard to the Jews, was influenced to a certain extent by the circles in which Tacitus and his associates moved.

The Early Christian Period. The anti-Semitism of the pagan world, whether expressed in outbreaks of violence and rioting or in ideological diatribes and libels, did not hold such fateful consequences for Jews as that which later crystallized within Christianity. The crucial factor here was not so much Christianity's refusal to countenance any other faith, as its commitment to an idea of redemption so manifestly in opposition to that of the Jews as to render their mutual coexistence inconceivable. With the political triumph of Christianity, the old pagan anti-Semitic image of the Jews as a people hated by God was resuscitated, but the reasons for God's hatred were changed to suit the new circumstances. Under the stigma of this image, the Jews were gradually excluded from every sphere of political influence and their political and civic rights were increasingly denied them, until in the end such rights were almost entirely a thing of the past.

Since Christianity originated as a dissident Jewish sect, certain judgments of Judaism in the New Testament must be examined in this light. Such, for instance, is the case with the writings of Saul (Paul) of Tarsus. In his Epistle to the Romans he protests against the idea of God's rejection of the Jews: "They are beloved for the sake of their forefathers" (Rom. 11:28): "I myself am an Israelite, a descendant of Abraham, a member of the tribe of Benjamin" (Rom. 11:1). Of the Gospels—easily the most popular writings in the New Testament—the last chronologically, namely Matthew and John, are the most hostile to Judaism, which they criticize from the standpoint of an outsider. In addition, these Gospels already contain the two cardinal themes appearing in Christian anti-Semitism: the Jews themselves are made to admit their collective responsibility for the crucifixion of the son of God ("Then answered all the people and said, His blood be on us, and on our children": Matt. 27:25), and are identified with the powers of evil ("Ye are of your father the devil, and your will is to do your father's desires": John 8:44).

Regarded by the Jews as members of a heretical sect, the

Christians stood aloof from the Jewish struggle against Rome. The Gospels' description of the 'crucifixion, in minimizing the role of Pilate,[13] attests a desire to gain the goodwill of the Roman authorities, while the destruction of Jerusalem in 70 C.E. provided obvious proof of the divine anger and chastisement. In sum, the evolution of Christian anti-Semitism reflects the spread of the new faith among pagan circles and a progressive withdrawal from the ancient faith. The growing hostility was also fed by the rivalry for proselytes. Since traditional Judaism continued to attract pagan elements, the newly Christianized groups were highly susceptible to its influence. The young church, therefore, which declared itself to be the true Israel, or "Israel according to the spirit," heir to the divine promises, found it essential to discredit the "Israel according to the flesh," to prove that God had cast away His people and transferred His love to the Christians. From the outset, therefore, Christian anti-Semitism was an original manifestation: it differed from the traditional tensions between Israel and the nations and did not merely reflect them. Obliged to contest Israel's historic heritage and title, and confronted in addition by a vigorous rabbinical counter-propaganda, the church unremittingly concentrated its attention on the Jews and Judaism. The anti-Jewish theories developed by the Church Fathers are preeminently variations or extensions of the first accusations leveled in the Gospels. They are developed with particular vehemence by the Greek Fathers who exercised their apostolic authority in regions where the Jewish population was large and influential. Certain polemics already afford an insight into the psychology of the early bishops, whose judeophobia was on the same scale as their religious fervor. To Gregory of Nyssa and John Chrysostom, love of Jesus and hatred for his presumed executioners were indistinguishable. These polemics also testify to the existence of a Jewish population which mixed with its Gentile neighbors on an equal footing. In the fourth

12 [13] Roman procurator of Judea 26–36 C.E.

century, John Chrysostom characteristically reproached these Jews with extravagance, gluttony, and dissolute living, as well as with deicide.

After Christianity became the official religion of the Roman state (321) the emperors began to translate the concepts and claims of the theologians into practice. The ancient privileges granted to the Jews were withdrawn, rabbinical jurisdiction was abolished or severely curtailed, and proselytism was prohibited and made punishable by death, as were relations with Christian women. Finally, Jews were excluded from holding high office or pursuing a military career. The rapid disintegration of the Roman Empire in the fifth century, however, postponed the principal effects of this legal forfeiture of rights. As the model that was to inspire the clerical and lay legislators of the Middle Ages, its repercussions on Judeo-Christian relations only become apparent centuries later. The persistence of Judaism, seemingly a contradiction of the Christian conception of the church as *Verus Israel*, "the true Israel," led the great theologians, notably Augustine, to elaborate the doctrine that represents the Jews as the nation which was a "witness" to the truth of Christianity. Their existence was further justified by the service they rendered to the Christian truth in attesting through their humiliation the triumph of the church over the synagogue. "Unintelligent, they possess intelligent books"; they are thus condemned to perpetual servitude. A further variation, reversing a biblical image, depicts the Jews as Esau and the Christians as Jacob. They are also Cain, guilty of fratricide, and marked with a sign. However, the hostility of this allegorization also implies a nascent tendency on the part of the church to protect the Jews, since "if someone killed Cain, Cain would be revenged sevenfold." Thus the ideological arsenal of Christian anti-Semitism was completely established in antiquity. However, from the social standpoint the deterioration of the Jewish position was only beginning, and it seems clear that in the early period virulent judeophobia was mainly limited to the clergy. 13

In Islam. From the theological standpoint, the Koran also contained attacks against the Jews, as they refused to recognize Muhammad as the prophet sent by God. In certain respects, Muhammad utilized the Bible in a manner similar to that of the Christian theologians, since he found in it the announcement of his own coming, but he also used the New Testament in the same way. As a result, Jews and Christians, although "infidels," are both regarded by the Koran as "Peoples of the Book," "possessing Scriptures."

Since Islam spread by force of arms rather than by spiritual propaganda, it did not generally aspire, at least initially, to conquer souls. Therefore, it displayed greater tolerance than Christianity. The religions of the two "Peoples of the Book" were officially recognized, and a special status combining subjection and protection was evolved for them. Apart from the distinguishing colors of their insignia, the *dhimmi* ("protected") Jews and Christians were subjected to the same measures and were obliged to pay the same tax. On various occasions they were included in the same persecutions. But in the regions where Islam reigned, the forms of anti-Judaism and anti-Christianity each evolved in their own way. When Islam began to spread, the majority of the subjected territories were Christian, and in them Greek remained the official language for some time. One source of anti-Semitism in Islam, therefore, may derive from ancient Christian anti-Semitism. The celebrated controversialist Al-Jahiz (mid-ninth century) cites in an anti-Christian polemic four reasons why the faithful held a better opinion of the Christians than of the Jews: the Christians wielded power in Byzantium and elsewhere; unlike the Jews, they engaged in secular sciences; they assimilated more easily and adopted Muslim names, and they engaged in more respectable occupations. In the same period the historian Al-Tabari observed that "the Christians bear witness against the Jews morning and night." Thus, a number of anti-Jewish traditions and legends from Christian folklore penetrated, with appropriate adaptations, into that of Islam.

However, the concepts relating to ritual purity and dietary laws, of similar inspiration for both Jews and Muslims, as well as the observance of circumcision, drew them together in that they excluded or lessened certain inhibitory phobias such as the fear of pollution. In addition, Muslim revelation was not founded on the biblical canon and could not become a ground of contention, thus excluding one source of polemics and oppression. In sum, the term anti-Semitism, which becomes a particularly blatant semantic misnomer when used in connection with the Arab world, also regarded as "Semitic", can be employed only with qualifications in reference to Islam.

From the 12th century, the expeditions of the Crusades aggravated the condition of Christians in the Orient. Persecutions were followed by forced mass conversions to Islam. In many regions the Jews remained the only "infidels" with exceptional status, so that their situation became more vulnerable. In North Africa and Muslim Spain they were also fiercely persecuted (period of the Almohads[14]). Yet it is from this period that the position of the Jews in western Christendom progressively deteriorated, and until the modern era, Jewish migration usually proceeded from Christian to Islamic countries. But migratory phenomena, like the frequency or intensity of persecutions, are imperfect indicators of a collective attitude. Literature provides a better conspectus. Although in Islamic literature and folklore the Jew is often depicted in an unfavorable light—frequently accused of malevolence toward non-Jews, or even of plotting their damnation—he is only in exceptional cases invested with the satanic character and attributes frequent in Christian literature. There are Islamic literary sources in the medieval age in which the contemporary Jew is endowed with positive characteristics. In the modern period the position of the Jew in Islamic countries, although varying according to region and historical circumstance, has tended to deteriorate. The

[14] A religious Muslim and political movement that was active in N.W. Africa and Spain in the 12th and 13th centuries

most notorious persecutions, in Yemen in 1697, and in Meshed, Iran in 1839, were perpetrated by Shi'ites. The *Yahud* confined to his ghetto—until recently in Yemen and even now in certain *mellahs* in Morocco—appeared to the Muslim an object of contempt rather than of hatred.

The Middle Ages. Jews had appeared in Western Europe from the beginning of the Christian era. At the commencement of the Middle Ages, no sign of singular animosity toward them was discernible. The clerical anti-Jewish polemics of the period deplored the influence the Jews exerted on the people, and pointed to the existence of cordial, sometimes intimate, Judeo-Christian relations. Characteristic are the epistles of the ninth-century Christian reformer Archbishop *Agobard: "Things have reached a stage where ignorant Christians claim that the Jews preach better than our priests . . . some Christians even celebrate the Sabbath with the Jews and violate the holy repose of Sunday . . . Men of the people, peasants, allow themselves to be plunged into such a sea of errors that they regard the Jews as the only people of God, and consider that they combine the observance of a pure religion and a truer faith than ours."

The Church Councils continually legislated to prevent these contacts. Ecclesiastical propaganda seems to have produced its first fruits at the beginning of the 11th century, when persecutions and expulsions were recorded in Rouen, Orleans, Limoges, and Mainz. A persecution inflicted at the time on Christians in the Orient was used as a pretext, and, apparently dating from the same period is the fable depicting the Jews as legionaries of the Anti-Christ. However, the crucial event was the First Crusade (1096). Religious excitation commingled with greed for gain. As bands of crusaders set out to recapture the sepulcher of Jesus they were prompted to wreak vengeance on Jesus' legendary enemies, and attacked the Jewish quarters of German and French towns along their way. The massacres perpetrated during the summer of 1096 made a lasting impression on both Christians and Jews. The tradition of sacrifice, *Kiddush ha-Shem*, was expressed in collective suicides to avoid forced conversion.

European economic life began to revive in the 12th century. Although the Christian guilds which began to flourish in the cities did not admit Jews, an action which had unfavorable repercussions on their commercial activities, the economic resurgence in Europe considerably increased credit operations, against which the church began to adopt measures. The church regarded the practice of usury as endangering the eternal salvation of its flock, and opposed the overt and authorized practice of usury, i.e., the acceptance of pledges, with particular severity. Being inevitable in contemporary economic conditions, however, the church subsequently endorsed the practice of usury by the Jews, for according to the prevalent opinion their souls were lost in any case. The doctrine and practice which thus spread constituted a major source of anti-Semitism for, in general, agrarian societies tended to leave the practice of usury to foreigners (those who were not "brothers"). The Jew, already stigmatized as an infidel and deicide, was now regarded by most as the direct antagonist of the Christian, and thus began to symbolize the hostile stranger *par excellence.* The process of differentiation was slow, as shown by the legend of a miraculous conversion around 1220 which places the following question in the mouth of a little girl: "Why is it that the Jews and the Christians have different names since they speak the same language and wear the same clothes?" Thus the Jew was distinguished primarily by his name, and in contemporary idiom the verb "to judaize" meant both to be a heretic and to lend money on interest.

Secular princes and church prelates were in fact the Jews' silent partners in the practice of usury. Although this partnership multiplied the sources of internal antagonism among Christians, the Jews were assured of an influential protection justified by patristic doctrines: the monarchs of the Holy Roman Empire regarded the Jews as serfs of the 17 chamber (*servi camerae*). Thomas Aquinas[15] considered them condemned to perpetual servitude because of their crime, but they were not to be deprived of the necessities of life. As a later scholastic, Angelo di Chivasso (1411–1495), said: "to be a Jew is a crime, not, however, punishable by a Christian."

Each renewed preaching for the Crusades roused anti-Jewish excesses, despite the protection afforded by the ecclesiastical and lay authorities. Religious consciousness in the masses intensified, and the evolution of theological thinking tended to emphasize and particularize the Jewish role as the scapegoat of Christianity. The 12th and 13th centuries saw the crystallization of the doctrine of transubstantiation, whereby the flesh and blood of Christ become present in the consecrated Host and wine—a doctrine definitively stated at the Fourth Lateran Council (1215). As a result, the eucharistic cult acquired concrete character. Miraculous tales in connection with the Host proliferated, frequently of Host desecration by the Jews, and the blood libel also began to inflict its ravages. These two closely connected allegations both relate to the delusion that a criminal conspiracy was being fabricated by the Jews against Jesus and the Christians. Psychologists have explained this suspicion as the transference of a guilt complex on the part of communicants. In partaking of the flesh and blood, they sought to identify themselves with the God-man who had taken upon himself the sins of the world, but they were unable to attain this identification satisfactorily. The resultant feeling of culpability could well be projected onto the "witness" people: the Jews were the people of God, but the only group to remain outside the universal communion of Christians.

The Fourth Lateran Council also promulgated a canon requiring the Jews to wear a distinguishing mark: the decision was intended to make any intimate relations between Jews and Christians impossible. The form of mark

18   [15] Christian medieval philosopher (1225–1274)

S. CORPO DEL B. SIMONE INNOCENTE E MARTIRE
CHE SI VENERA NELLA CHIESA DEI SS. APOSTOLI PIETRO E PAOLO
IN TRENTO

Memorial card distributed until recent years in the cathedral in Trent, where Simon's relics are preserved. See p. 75.

was not specified. In practice, the Jews in Latin countries were made to adopt a disk sewn onto their clothing, and in the Germanic countries a distinctive hat. Characteristically, contemporary iconography also depicts the biblical patriarchs, as well as Christian heretics of all kinds, in this dress. The appearance of the Jewish badge also helped to propagate fables that showed the Jews as physically different from other men. Other features ascribed include a tail and horns—the attributes of the devil—and a distinctive smell *(foetor judaicus),* the converse of "the odor of sanctity."

During the 13th century the economic position of the Jews, and consequently the protection from which they benefited, was impaired by the development of finance on an international scale in Italy by, e.g., the Florentine and Siennese banks, and by the Lombards in France. The kings of England found that they could now dispense with the services of the Jews, and expelled them in 1290. In 1306 the first general expulsion from France took place. Expulsions 19

The earliest known English portrayal of a Jew is this carica-
ture dated 1277 and entitled "Aaron, son of the Devil." He
wears the badge used in England to distinguish Jews—the
tablets of the Law. London, Public Record Office.

and massacres also followed in the German towns. The
mass expulsions helped to perpetuate the image of Jewish
homelessness, of the Wandering Jew condemned to roam
from country to country, in the eyes of the masses. At the
beginning of the 14th century the specter of conspiracy
against Christianity found new expression in the popular

belief that the wells were being poisoned by the Jews. It is necessary to draw a distinction between these myths of a popular demonology, which the church itself did not endorse, but on the contrary combated, and the clerical anti-Jewish tradition. Apart from the religious and economic factors referred to above, persistent agencies of religious excitation were the development of a literature written in the vernacular and the growing popularity of the "Passion plays," which reenacted the crucifixion. Passion plays took place annually, lasted several days, and presented the cruelty and perfidy of the Jewish executioners in a highly realistic fashion.

Very often the established lay and ecclesiastical authorities continued to protect the Jews The most implacable adversaries of the Jews were now recruited among the rising middle class, and particularly among the mendicant Franciscan and Dominican orders. The Italian anti-Jewish Franciscan preachers John of Capistrano and Bernardino da Feltre, at whose instigation the institution of the *Monte di Pietà* [16] spread rapidly, and the Dominican Vincente Ferrer in Spain, were especially vituperative. In Spain, the slow pace of the Christian reconquest—a process lasting from the 11th to the 15th centuries—enabled the Jews to continue to benefit from a privileged situation. Thus the conceptions current in the rest of Europe took time to spread to the Peninsula. It was not until the end of the 14th century that the preaching of Archdeacon Fernando Martinez of Seville set in motion a wave of bloody persecutions. The numerical and social importance of Spanish Jewry resulted in a different evolution, particularly the phenomenon of Crypto-Judaism practiced by the Conversos. [17] The Castilian Inquisition was founded in 1478 to eradicate it. In 1492 Jews of the faith were expelled from Spain after a preliminary blood libel trial—the case of Nino de la Guardia—had been staged.

[16] Public loan banks in N. Italy to replace Jewish moneylenders
[17] Term applied in Spain and Portugal to converted Jews

Poland, where a Christian middle class was slow to develop, became the principal country of refuge for European Jewry at the end of the Middle Ages. Russia, however, followed a different course in consequence of a religious schism which menaced Russian Orthodoxy at the end of the 14th century. This "judaizing heresy" predicated in an extreme form the tendencies of return to the Old Testament present in the Reformation movements of Western Europe. It acquired followers at the court of Moscow but was rapidly stifled. As a result, access to Russia was barred to Jews hereafter. Religious struggle was thus the starting point for the traditional judeophobia of the ruling Russian dynasties.

In general, popular susceptibility to anti-Semitism developed in the Middle Ages. It was henceforth perpetuated by linguistic usage and religious instruction. In all languages the term "Jew" and its derivatives had assumed a derogatory significance. Religious instruction by the catechism, practically the only form of popular education until a later period, instilled hostility against the "executioners of Christ" into the souls of children. "If it is incumbent upon a good Christian to detest the Jews, then we are all good Christians," Erasmus stated ironically at the beginning of the 16th century.

The Reformation. The Reformation had important complex and even contradictory repercussions on the evolution of anti-Semitism. One branch of Protestantism, namely Calvinism and the sects or movements influenced by it, proved less judeophobic than Catholicism until the 20th century. The other branch, Lutheranism, became increasingly anti-Semitic. How may this divergency be explained? It is as difficult to give a complete answer as it is to establish the exact relationship, a problem posed by Max Weber[18] and his school, between the "Protestant ethic" and "the capitalist spirit" or modern mentality. From the outset Calvinism and its derivatives emphasized individual re-

[18] German economist and sociologist (1864–1920)

sponsibility, embracing social values and energetic moral action. To Lutheranism, on the other hand, justification by faith implied a renunciation of civic responsibility, and hostility to active faith (or "salvation through works"), which Luther himself described as *juedischer Glaube* ("Jewish faith"). At the end of his life the German reformer vilified the Jews in violent pamphlets which could not fail to exert their influence. Conversely, the role played by the Old Testament in Calvinism led the Puritan sects to identify themselves with the Jews of the Bible and reflected favorably on their attitude toward contemporary Jewry. The French Calvinists were a special case: themselves persecuted until the French Revolution, their sympathies were traditionally pro-Jewish, an outlook retained to a considerable extent to the present day.

An immediate consequence of the Reformation was to aggravate the position of the Jews in regions which remained Catholic. The popes of the Counter-Reformation were determined to restore ecclesiastical usages and the strict application of canon law. One result was that from the second half of the 16th century ghettos were introduced, at first in Italy and afterward in the Austrian Empire. This segregation then served as a convenient additional demonstration of the error of Judaism: "A Jewish ghetto is a better proof of the truth of the religion of Jesus Christ than a whole school of theologians," declared the 18th-century Catholic publicist G. B. Roberti. In France, the celebrated Bossuet had expressed analogous views in the 17th century. With the advent of the Counter-Reformation, therefore, the theses of Augustine and Thomas Aquinas regarding the Jews were applied to the letter. However, in the Low Countries, which had been freed of Spanish domination, the Jews could settle freely. They also began to settle in Great Britain and its colonies, and in particular North America, from the time of Cromwell.

Spain after 1492. Traditional Christian conceptions condemned the Jews because their faith was erroneous and strenuous efforts were made to convert them, but the mass 23 conversion in Spain in the 15th century resulted in transference of the customary hostility to the converts and their real or suspected descendants, the New Christians.[19] In other words, religious anti-Semitism, far from disarmed by the disappearance of Jews of the faith, transformed itself into racial anti-Semitism. The Inquisition gradually stamped out Crypto-Judaism. However, statutes promulgated in Spain made "purity of blood" *(limpieza de sangre)* a new criterion to bar entry of the New Christians whose faith was suspect, to certain guilds, and to certain military and religious orders. This discrimination, sanctioned by Emperor Charles V, spread to the military academies and universities and persisted until the Napoleonic Wars. The law involved detailed genealogical research, and contributed to the obsession with the code of honor and hidalgoism characteristic of old-time Spain. Since New Christians were traditionally concentrated in productive and commercial occupations and in crafts, the contempt with which they were held was connected with these callings. Such an attitude can be considered a major cause of Spanish economic decline in modern times. Vestiges of this attitude toward the New Christians still persist in the Balearic islands, affecting the Chuetas[20] of Palma de Majorca. Needless to say, the determinant of "purity of blood" was not based on actual religious, cultural, or even biological differences, but on the illusion fostered by the Old Christians that such a difference existed.

The Enlightenment. For as long as Christianity held unchallenged sway in Europe, Jews could exist only on the margin of European social life. With the coming of the 18th-century Enlightenment, however, their isolation slowly began to crumble. A new class of bourgeois intellectuals—the *philosophes*—denounced Christianity in the name of Deism, or "natural religion," and ushered in the

---

[19] Term applied especially in Spain and Portugal to converts from Judaism and their descendants

[20] Term of abuse referring to Marranos of Majorca

secularism of the modern era. As a result of their efforts, for the first time in centuries the status of the Jews became a matter for widespread debate. Many *philosophes* found it only natural to sympathize with the Jews. Not only were Jews the oppressed people *par excellence* in a century which prided itself on its concern for justice, but they were also the most notorious victims of Christian intolerance, which the Enlightenment was sworn to destroy. Accordingly, protests against the persecution of Jews—and especially against the Inquisition, the Enlightenment's *bête noire*—became one of the standard set pieces of 18th-century rhetoric. Led by Montesquieu, Lessing,[21] and Rousseau, Enlightenment writers everywhere preached that Christian and Jew shared a common humanity and common human rights. Relatively few of these men foresaw the Emancipation, which for most of the 18th century remained a distant prospect. But emancipation was proposed as early as 1714 by the English freethinker John Toland, and it drew increasing support from *philosophes* as the century went on. When, at last, the Jews of France were emancipated in 1791, it was largely the authority of the Enlightenment which overcame the objections of churchmen and gentile economic interests.

Despite its achievements, however, the Enlightenment's pro-Jewish agitation was not so purely humanitarian as it appeared. Much of the indignation which Jewish suffering aroused was calculated not to comfort the Jews, but to exploit their plight for the purpose of condemning Christianity. Admiring accounts of the Jewish religion, such as those favored by Lessing, were also intended to discredit Christianity—often so blatantly that, like Lessing's famous *Nathan der Weise,* they expounded Judaism as a religion for *philosophes* to make Christianity seem backward by comparison. In short, when the Enlightenment chose to defend the Jews, it did so largely for reasons of its own; and it dealt with them, in consequence, not as real individuals, but as a useful abstraction. The sole novelty of its approach

---

[21] German dramatist, philosopher, and critic (1729–1781)

was that, whereas the Jews had once been a witness to the truth of Christianity, now they were expected to demonstrate its error. The actual Jews, meanwhile, were usually regarded with suspicion and distaste. The Judaism which they practiced, after all, was a religion much like Christianity and hence to the Enlightenment a "superstition" to be eradicated. What was still more serious, Judaism was often considered a particularly anti-social religion, one which nurtured a stubborn sense of particularism and created grave divisions within the state. These opinions were so widely held by Enlightenment writers that even friends of the Jews continually urged them to abandon their traditions and observances. Only Montesquieu, of all the 18th century's great thinkers, showed any willingness to accept the Jews without reforming them into something else. Indeed, the most common argument for emancipation, as conceived by Dohm, Mirabeau, and others, was precisely that it would convert the Jews to the majority culture, thus expunging their most obnoxious traits. This view was ultimately upheld by the French revolutionaries, who declared, when they emancipated the Jews in 1791: "To the man, everything; to the Jew, nothing." Though as a citizen the Jew was to receive full rights, as a Jew he was to count for nothing.

Even so, this program of compulsory emancipation did not fully reflect the intense Jew-hatred of the more extreme *philosophes.* Though it is surprising to recall the fact, among this group were some of the leading minds of the 18th century, including Diderot, d'Holbach, and Voltaire. Despite their intellectual stature, these men launched scurrilous attacks on the Jews which far surpassed the bounds of reasoned criticism. Many of their polemics were not only intolerant, but so vicious and spiteful as to compare with all but the crudest propaganda of our own day. To some extent, this anti-Jewish fervor can be understood as merely one aspect of the Enlightenment's war on Christianity. Diderot, d'Holbach, Voltaire, and their followers were the most radical anti-Christians of their time, and—in contrast to the more moderate Deists who praised the Jews—they did not hesitate to pour scorn on Christianity by reviling its Jewish origins. This tactic was all the more useful because Judaism, unlike Christianity, could be abused in print without fear of prosecution; but even the fact that the Jews made a convenient whipping-boy cannot explain all the hostility which they excited. "Enlightened" diatribes against Jews were often so bitter, so peculiarly violent, that they can only have stemmed from a profound emotional antagonism—a hatred nourished not only by dislike of Jewish particularism, refurbished from ancient Greco-Roman sources, but also by unconscious Christian prejudice and resentment of Jewish economic success. Voltaire, in particular, detested the Jews with vehement passion. A large part of his whole enormous output was devoted to lurid tales of Jewish credulity and fanaticism, which he viewed as dangerous threats to European culture. At times, Voltaire actually pressed this argument so far as to imply that Jews were ignorant by nature, and could never be integrated into a modern society.

To be sure, racist ideas of this kind made little headway against the ingrained egalitarianism of the Enlightenment. Neither Voltaire nor any other pre-Revolutionary thinker seriously denied that Jews could be assimilated, so that in this sense, at least, anti-Semitism was hardly known. Still less respectable were outright fantasies like the blood libel, which most Enlightenment writers firmly repudiated. Yet the fact remains that, for all their resistance to racism and other delusions, some of the leaders of the Enlightenment played a central role in the development of anti-Semitic ideology. By declaring the Jew an enemy of the modern secular state, they refurbished the anti-Semitism of the Middle Ages and set it on an entirely new path. In so doing, moreover, they revealed a depth of feeling against Jews which was wholly disproportionate to the Jews' supposed faults, and which would continue to inspire anti-Semitism even when the Jews' secularism was no longer open to question. 27

Emancipation and Reaction. The newer 19th-century version of anti-Semitism arose on a soil which had been watered for many centuries in Europe by Christian theology and, more important, by popular catechisms. The Christian centuries had persecuted Jews for theological reasons, but this "teaching of contempt" had set the seal on the most ancient of all anti-Semitic themes: that the Jews were a uniquely alien element within human society. In every permutation of European politics and economics within the course of the century, the question of the alienness of the Jew reappeared as an issue of quite different quality from all of the other conflicts of a stormy age. Jews themselves tended to imagine that their troubles represented the time-lag of older, medieval Christian attitudes, of the anger at "Christ-killers" and "Christ-rejecters," which would eventually disappear. It was not until the work of Leo Pinsker and Theodor Herzl, the founders of modern Zionism, that the suggestion was made that anti-Semitism in all of its varieties was, at its very root, a form of xenophobia, the hatred of a stranger—the oldest, most complicated, and most virulent example of such hatred— and that the end of the medieval era of faith and politics did not, therefore, mean the end of anti-Semitism.

As a result of both the French and the American revolutions there were two major states in the world at the beginning of the 19th century in which, in constitutional theory, Jews were now equal citizens before the law. (The Jews of Holland, as a result of the French conquest there, were also granted emancipation in 1796). In neither case was their emancipation complete. In the U.S. certain legal disabilities continued to exist in some of the individual states and the effort for their removal encountered some re-echoes of older Christian prejudices. The Jews in America were, however, at the beginning of the 19th century a mere handful, less than 3,000 in a national population approaching 4,000,000, and there was therefore no contemporary social base for the rise of a serious anti-Semitic reaction. The issues were different in Europe. In France there had been more than a century of conflict between Jewish smallscale moneylenders, illegal artisans, and petty creditors and their gentile clients and competitors. The legal emancipation of the Jews did not still these angers but, on the contrary, exacerbated them. The spokesmen of the political left in eastern France during the era of the Revolution and even into the age of Napoleon argued, without exception that the new legal equality for the Jews would not act to assimilate them as "useful and productive citizens" into the main body of the French people but, rather that it would open new avenues for the rapacity of these aliens. Napoleon's own activities in relation to the Jewish question, including the calling of his famous French Sanhedrin[22] in 1807, were under the impact of two themes: the desire to make the Jews assimilate more rapidly and the attempt, through a decree that announced a ten-year moratorium on debts owed to Jews in eastern France, to calm the angers of their enemies. On the other hand, Jews were visibly and notoriously the beneficiaries of the Revolution. It was, indeed, true that a number of distinguished émigrés had been helped to escape by former associates who were Jews, and it was even true that the bulk of the Jewish community, at least at the very beginning of the Revolution and a few years later during the Terror, feared rather than favored the new regime. Nonetheless, in the minds of the major losers, the men of the old order and especially of the church, the Jews were the chief, or at the very least the most obvious, winners during the era of the Revolution. The association of French anti-Semitism with counterrevolutionary forces, with royalist-clericalist reaction, throughout the next 150 years was thus begun very early. In the demonology of anti-Semitism it was not difficult to transform the Sanhedrin in Paris in 1807 into a meeting of a secret society of Jews plotting to take over the world. This connection was made in that year by Abbé Barruel in his book *Mémoire pour servir a l'histoire du*

---

[22] Body of representative Jews convoked by Napoleon in 1807

jacobinisme. This volume is the source of all of the later elaborations of the myth of the Elders of Zion.

In Europe as a whole a new kind of anti-Semitism was evoked by the new kind of war that the revolutionary armies, and the far more successful armies of Napoleon, were waging against their enemies. Between 1790 and 1815 the armies of France appeared everywhere not, as they announced, as conquerors holding foreign territory for ransom or for annexation, but as liberators of the peoples from the yoke of their existing governments in order to help them regenerate themselves in a new state of freedom. Wherever the Revolution spread, its legislation included, in places as far-flung as Westphalia, Italy, and even briefly, Erez Israel, equality for Jews. It was entirely reasonable on the part of the Austrian police, and the secret services of some of the other European powers, to suspect that some of the Jews within their borders were really partisans of Napoleon. In the wake of his defeat the emancipation of the Jews remained on the books in France, but it was removed elsewhere, with some modifications in favor of Jews, as an imposition of a foreign power. The battle for Jewish equality had to begin again; it became part of a century-long battle in Europe to achieve the liberal revolution everywhere. This struggle had not yet ended by the time of World War I, for at that moment the largest Jewish community in the world, that in the Russian Empire, was not yet emancipated and had, indeed, suffered grievously throughout the century.

In the early and middle years of the 19th century the most important battleground between Jews and their enemies was in Germany. Capitalism was rapidly remaking the social structure and Jews were the most easily identifiable element among the "new men." The victims of the rising capitalist order, especially the lower-middle classes, found their scapegoat in the most vulnerable group among the successful, the Jews. In a different part of society, and from a nationalist perspective, the most distinguished of German historians of the day, Heinrich

Treitschke, was insisting toward the end of the century that the acculturated and legally emancipated Jews, who thought in their own minds that they had become thoroughly German, were really aliens who still had to remake themselves from the ground up and to disappear inconspicuously. Not long after the turn of the century Werner Sombart (*Die Juden und das Wirtschaftsleben,* 1911) was to express his own ambivalence about capitalism as a whole by insisting, against Max Weber, that it was the Jews, and not the Protestants, who had always been, even in biblical days, the inventors and bearers of the capitalist spirit. Such identification between the Jews and the spirit of capitalism had been made, to their discredit, seven decades earlier, in 1844, by the young Karl Marx in his essay "On the Jewish Question." For anti-Semites of both the political right and the left, who hated capitalism for different reasons, such identification was one of the sources and rationales of Jew-hatred throughout the modern era, into the Nazi period. Hatreds rooted in class conflict combined with angers which derived from visions of national and cultural authenticity to produce the most violent and murderous attack on Jews in all history.

On the surface of events modern German anti-Semitism began with riots by the peasants in 1819, using the rhetoric of older Christian hatreds. This hatred of Jews was soon transformed by the rising romanticism and the nationalist reactions to the Napoleonic wars into an assertion that the true German spirit, which had arisen in the Teutonic forests, was an organic and lasting identity in which the Jew could not, by his very nature, participate. For this purpose the work of Gobineau[23] on race was pressed into service to make the point that the Jews were a non-Aryan, Oriental element whose very nature was of a different modality. Richard Wagner[24] insisted on this point not only in his overt anti-Semitic utterances but also indirectly in his operas, in

[23] French diplomat and essayist (1816–1882)
[24] German composer and racial theoretician (1813–1883)

which he crystallized the Teutonic myths as a quasi-religious expression of the authentic German spirit. In Wagner's footsteps there appeared the work of his son-in-law, Houston Stewart Chamberlain (*The Foundations of the Nineteenth Century*, 1899), which pronounced the presence of Jews in German society to be radically inimical to its very health. In the popular mind these theorists of national culture were understood within a situation in which the intellectual importance of Germany in Europe was not equaled by its political significance, for the scandalous division of the country lasted until 1870. To be united and German was the dominant ideal.

The very difficulties in realizing the unity of Germany brought the existence of Jews into unfriendly focus. Very few elements in mid-19th century Germany society, even among their friends, were willing to regard Jews as true Germans. Jews were asking for political equality more in the name of the universal rights of man—that is, as partisans of the cosmopolitan principle—than as sons of the German people. As a result, the ultimate attainment of equality, first in Prussia in 1859 and ultimately in all of Germany in the aftermath of the unification of the country in 1870, had a quite narrow social base. It was identified with the rise of the bourgeois liberalism, but this element never dominated in mid-19th-century Germany as it did in contemporary England. What was worse, from a Jewish perspective, was that as a middle-class element the Jews were themselves in competition with the very class which had facilitated their entry into society. Toward the end of the century the German middle class itself was shifting its political alignment from liberalism to romantic conservatism. To be sure, the main thrust of German liberalism continued to regard anti-Semitism as reactionary, just as the main body of German Socialism would have no truck with the identification of all Jews with the capitalist oppressors of the working class. Nonetheless, anti-Semitism was sufficiently potent for all its themes to coalesce into the

image of the successful, non-national, unproductive foreigner, whose power resided in money and in his mastery of the legerdermain of modern manipulation. This "Jew" was a lineal descendant of the Jewish maker of love potions in Greco-Roman demonology and the poisoner of wells of the medieval myths, but the new version was very up to date and answered to contemporary frustrations and angers.

In the last quarter of the 19th century, anti-Semitism became an acceptable element in German political life to be manipulated at opportune moments by political leaders seeking popular lower-middle-class support. The very term anti-Semitism had been invented by Wilhelm Marr in 1879 and it was in that year that the court chaplain, Adolph Stoecker, had made his first public anti-Semitic speech, "Our Demands on Moden Judaism," and had then turned his Christian Socialist Party into overtly anti-Jewish directions. With the rise of German imperialism toward the end of the century and the sense of success it gave Germany, political anti-Semitism waned, but social distance continued unaltered.

In France, Jews had not been an issue of any considerable importance after the restoration of the Bourbons to power in 1815. There alone Jewish political gains had been safeguarded without question, because the fundamental social changes which had been introduced by the Revolution could not be radically altered by the return of the émigrés. Nonetheless, Jews remained one of the most visible symbols of these very changes, and the attacks upon Jews, both from the extreme right and the extreme left, were sufficiently overt to provide the spark for greater difficulties in the second half of the century. Two of the greatest theorists of Socialism in France, Proudhon and Fourier, were anti-Jewish on the ground that Jewish capitalist interests stood counter to those of the peasants and the workers, and that the Jewish spirit as a whole was antithetical to their vision of a reformed humanity living the life of unselfish social justice. In France, too, the changes being brought about by capitalism and the Industrial Revolution made many people feel helpless, as their lives 33 were being remade for the worse. The power of the Rothschilds was very evident in France, especially in the age of Louis Napoleon, and some of the anger at the new age came to expression in attacks on them by left-wingers such as Toussenel. In the time of conflict which followed the fall of France in 1870 major elements among all forces contending for power after the debacle could blame their troubles on the Jews.

In the renewed political battles of the 1870s and 1880s the overwhelming majority of the Jewish community in France was associated with the liberal republican forces against the conservative Catholics, who were enemies of the Republic. From 1879 to 1884 republican anti-clericals dominated in parliament and succeeded in freeing French education from clerical control. One of the building blocks of the almost successful counterrevolution of 1888, in which General Boulanger very nearly made an end of the Republic, was anti-Semitism. The myth that the small handful of Jews in France had enormous and highly dangerous power had been broadcast two years before in perhaps the single, most successful anti-Semitic and counterrevolutionary book ever published, Edouard Drumont's *La France Juive,* which went through innumerable editions. Late in 1894 anti-Semitism became the central issue of French society and politics for at least a decade and the reechoes of the positions taken in those years can still be heard. Captain Alfred Dreyfus, the first Jew to become a member of the general staff of the French army, was accused of spying for Germany. The outcry against Dreyfus was joined not only by the clerical-royalist right but also by some elements of the French left. His ultimate vindication was the result of the exercise of moral conscience in the service of truth by a number of individuals more concerned about the preservation of the Republic than about the rights of Jews.

Russia and Central Europe. There was a radical difference between the situation in Western Europe in the 19th century and that which prevailed in the Russian Empire. At least in theory the West European states were not anti-Jewish.

34

Despite occasional liberalizations, the czarist regime as a whole regarded it as its duty to protect the bulk of its population against the spread of Jewish economic influence or even of Jewish population. A few attempts in the course of the century at the assimilation of the Jews did not alter the basic outlook of the state, that Jews were dangerous aliens. The czar continued to derive the validation of his absolutism from theology, from the identification of the caesar and Jesus by the Orthodox faith; anti-Semitism based on Christian religious prejudice thus remained alive and virulent. Whatever hopes the Jews had in the course of the 19th century for improvement in their status rested in the hopes for the evolution of czarist absolutism toward parliamentary democracy. Repeated repressions made such hopes clearly illusory, and younger Jews in increasing numbers turned to helping to prepare revolution. This served to enrage the government, and the reactionary circles which supported it, even further. The regime kept imposing more economic disabilities on the Jews, keeping them in the least secure of middlemen occupations such as petty shopkeepers, innkeepers, and managers of estates for absentee landlords; in these capacities Jews were in direct, often unpleasant, contact with the poorest of the peasants. The government made it its business to use these resentments to draw attention away from the seething angers which pervaded the whole of the social system. Anti-Semitism was thus encouraged and fostered as a tactical tool for preserving czarist absolutism.

The critically important event in the history of Russian anti-Semitism took place in 1881, when a wave of pogroms occurred involving outbreaks in some 160 cities and villages of Russia. The occasion for these outrages was the assassination of Czar Alexander II by revolutionary terrorists on March 13, 1881. Among the assassins was one Jewish girl who played a quite minor role, but reactionary newspapers almost immediately began to whip up anti-Jewish sentiment. The government probably did not directly organize these riots, but it stood aside as Jews were

35

"Cast your vote for Kadet!!" ("Constitutional Democratic Party," a liberal party of the center). Front page of the Russian anti-Semitic weekly, Pluvium, 1907.

murdered and pillaged, and the regime used the immediate occasion to enact anti-Jewish economic legislation in 1882 (the May Laws). The situation continued to deteriorate to such a degree that in the next reign Czar Nicholas II gave money to the anti-Semitic organization, the Black Hundreds, and made no secret of his personal membership, and that of the crown prince, in that organization. This violent anti-Semitic movement was associated with the government in directly formenting pogroms during the revolutionary years of 1903 and 1905; in that latter year the *Protocols of the Elders of Zion* was published under the auspices of the secret police by the press of the czar, although he himself believed the work to be a fraud. The ordeal of Mendel Beilis arose within the hysterical atmosphere of disintegrating czarism. He was accused in 1911 in Kiev of ritual murder, and the full weight of government power was put behind the prosecution. His acquittal at the trial in 1913 was the culmination of two years of battle between the regime and the Jews and their supporters in liberal humanitarian circles in Russia and throughout the world.

It was, indeed, in such circles, which were the Russian parallel to the forces which had created western parliamentary democracy and social and intellectual liberalism, that the Jews found support during a tragic period. When these elements came briefly to power in the revolution of February 1917 the Jews were immediately given the rights of equal citizens. Nonetheless, despite this later, brief, and abortive victory of liberalism, after 1882 this current seemed too weak and divided to afford the Jews much hope for the future. Men like Turgenev[25] had mixed feelings about Jews and even Tolstoy[26] did not always hasten to support them when they were under attack. The political left was even more ambiguous. Even some of the Jews within the general revolutionary movements saw the Jewish petty bourgeoisie not as a victim but as an oppressor. The anger of the peasants and the urban poor was, therefore, regarded as merited, and their pogrom activities were even viewed as positive stirrings toward the ultimate revolution. This was, for example, the stand of the Narodniki, the

[25] Russian novelist (1818–1883)
[26] Russian novelist and social reformer (1828–1910)

pro-peasant populist group, with regard to the pogroms of 1881. More fundamentally, the revolutionary groups in Russia had even less patience with specifically Jewish problems, or with any desires on the part of Jews to continue their own communal identity, than was to be found in the European left as a whole. The young Lenin[27] was an opponent of anti-Semitism, and he held that the problems of the Jews would disappear along with that of all other people in Russia in a new socialist order. On the other hand, Lenin insisted that Jews would have to undergo a more radical and cultural transformation than any other element in Russia and that any Jew who opposed assimilation was "simply a nationalist philistine" ("The Position of the Bund[28] in the Party," in *Iskra,* Oct. 22, 1903). Any form of Jewish association of feeling had already been pronounced to be a form of particularly obnoxious reaction. The stage was thus set for the ultimate questioning by Stalin of the loyalty of even Communist Jews.

These difficulties in the Russian Empire in the decades right before and after 1900 had their parallels in the buffer countries between Germany and Russia. In Rumania, despite promises that had been made in the Berlin Convention of 1878, Jews were systematically excluded from most walks of life. Even the native born were declared to be foreigners, so that very few Jews held citizenship. There was little that Jews could do except attempt to flee in large numbers. In the Austro-Hungarian Empire the blood libel was revived in 1899 in Bohemia, but this was only the most sensational case of a series that had begun in Tisza-Eszlar, a small Hungarian village, in 1882. Much Jewish energy went into the defense against such charges. What was being debated was not so much the blatant lie of the blood accusation but rather the more fundamental issue of the moral integrity of Judaism and the Jew. This was, essentially, still medieval anti-Semitism, but more contem-

[27] Russian revolutionary, founder of the Soviet State (1870–1924)

[28] Jewish workers' movement in Russia, founded in 1897

porary currents were running strong. There were deep national tensions within the multinational Austro-Hungarian Empire, and the Jews were caught in the middle of all of the most embittered of these situations. In Bohemia they identified with the ruling Germans, to the chagrin and anger of Czech nationalists, but the local Germans nevertheless rejected the Jews as not true members of the *Volk*. In Galicia, the poorest and most medieval of the Austro-Hungarian provinces, the dominant Poles could claim a majority over the Ukrainians only by counting the Jews as Poles, but that did not induce them to accept even those Jews who were Polonizing themselves. The masses of Galician Jewry, almost a million at the turn of the century, were living in poverty that was abject even by Russian and Rumanian standards, with no hope of betterment.

Between East and West. Those years were the crucial turning point, the hinge on which modern Jewish history, the era of the emancipation, turned into contemporary Jewish history, the age of unparalleled virulence of anti-Semitism, the virtual end of European Jewry, and the rise of the American Jewish community and the State of Israel. Between 1880 and 1900 it became clear that the dominant response to the growing difficulties and dangers in Central and Eastern Europe was for Jews to attempt to flee westward; at first westward in Europe itself, to Vienna in the Austro-Hungarian Empire, to Germany, to France, and to England. In all of these countries quite small Jewish populations were, on the average, at least doubled between 1882 and 1914. In the United States, however, during that very same period, the Jewish population increased nearly fifteenfold, from a quarter of a million to three and a half million; Jews were some 8% of the total that arrived between 1880 and 1914. In the main, the reasons for this great increase were economic as America was then expanding rapidly in economic dynamism and through the settling of its large territories, and was thus in need of large numbers of new immigrants. However, a partial reason was the increasing lack of hospitality to Jews in Western Europe. Anti-Semitism was growing, and so was the increased fear of it on the part of the older Jewish residents in Germany, France, and England. In Vienna the 1890s were marked by the repeated reelection as mayor of the city of Karl Lueger on an avowedly anti-Semitic platform. Lueger appealed to the impoverished lower-middle classes, who envied the success of Jews in Vienna's economic and cultural life. The emperor refused to confirm his first three elections, but on the fourth such occasion, in 1897, he finally gave in. It was Lueger to whom the very young Adolf Hitler listened when he came to Vienna to try to become a painter; it was Lueger whom Theodor Herzl had in mind when, watching the degradation of Alfred Dreyfus in Paris, he came to the conclusion that anti-Semitism which could become a major political issue in the two most enlightened cities in Europe could no longer be regarded as a passing phenomenon. Even in England, the country which had been freest of all forms of anti-Semitism in the middle third of the 19th century, it reappeared after 1881, as relatively large numbers of Yiddish-speaking new immigrants continued to arrive. The moral qualities and working habits of these Jews were debated and investigated by parliamentary commissions and, after years of tension, an Aliens Act putting restrictions on further immigration became law in 1905.

In England, and even in France during the Dreyfus affair, anti-Jewish arguments and attitudes rested on a purely national premise, that is, on the supposed need to protect the integrity of national traditions. So, for example, the problem for Charles Maurras, the central figure of French integral nationalism, was whether the Jews would be regarded, along with Bretons, Normans, etc., as one of the valid "families of France." It was, indeed, to the nationalist forms of anti-Semitism that Pinsker and Herzl were responding by suggesting that the cure for such tensions could come through the establishment of a normalized Jewish national identity parallel to that of all other nations. In those years, however, new forms of anti-Semitism were arising. These were no longer rooted in real or supposed defense of national integrity. The ideologies of both Pan-Germanism and Pan-Slavism were politically conceived in international terms (both movements were in being in 1890). In the realm of metaphysics their sense of the Teutonic or Slavic traditions as the prime bearers of human culture reflected, and conflicted with, biblical notions about the chosenness of the Jews. The distance from either of these ideologies to racism, to the insistence that the superiority of the Slav or the German inhered not in his history but in his very biological type, was not very large. Gobineau, who had been half forgotten, was again being read in the 1890s, especially in Germany. The first international meeting of all the anti-Semitic parties of Europe had taken place as early as 1882; by 1900 anti-Semitism was clearly an international movement in which hatred of the Jews had become the unifying premise for groups as disparate and clashing as the anti-Dreyfusards and the nationalists of the very Germany for which Alfred Dreyfus had been accused of spying. This paradox made a certain kind of anti-Semitic sense. Jews were heavily identified in the major capitals of European culture with the most modern, critical, cosmopolitan supra-national spirit, and thus with the very cultural force which the newest ideologies of the radical right were trying to destroy. The leading figure of the Enlightenment, Voltaire, had not believed that Jews could ever really become *philosophes*, and he had, therefore, been less than a staunch proponent of their equality. Little more than a century later the newest forms of national anti-Semitism were attacking the Jews as harmful to society precisely because they were regarded, with considerable truth, as the most significant single element among the bearers of the tradition of the European Enlightenment. In this task Jews continued to be important in Europe after 1900, but their position was already clearly embattled, and the role was being abandoned, at least in part. By that year the Jewish masses on the move had already made a crucial decision that the future of most of the migrants was to be found in the United States. The ideologists and earliest pioneers of Zionism had moved eastward, out of the European arena to the creation of a renewed Jewish national identity in Erez Israel.

For the first two centuries of the United States' national history anti-Semitism as an active force was practically nonexistent. Certain remnants of exclusion on Christian grounds from public office did exist in the early years of the 19th century, but these were all ultimately removed on the grounds of constitutional logic. As a population the Jews were an insignificant handful; the social structure of the country as a whole was largely fluid. The serious conflicts within the United States until after the Civil War had almost nothing to do with Jews, and they played so little role that none of the contenders could use them as scapegoat. A certain amount of endemic social prejudice reappeared in 1870s, especially in the sight of the rapid economic rise of the first generation of German Jews to affluence. This was one expression of the process by which newly rich gentile elements were asserting their social positions by manufacturing exclusiveness. The serious tensions which did arise were a concomitant of the mass immigration from 1881 to 1914, as gentiles fled from—or battled to retain—neighborhoods becoming filled with masses of very foreign Jews from Eastern Europe. There was substantial discrimination in housing and educational opportunities at the colleges and universities, and especially in jobs in the highly structured bureaucracies of heavy industry, insurance, and banking. This new immigration provided in the first third of the century many of both the leaders and the followers of what little there was of left-wing politics in the big cities. This was well remembered in the reaction to the Russian Revolution and later, to the Great Depression of 1929, when there appeared a substantial amount of overt American anti-Semitism. This was carried further in the 1930s under the impetus of Nazism and its American wing, the German-American Bund.

Native-born American radicalism, the populist tradition

with its suspicions of the big cities, the intellectuals and, above all, of the Wall Street bankers, had its own anti-Semitic component. It looked for a moment in the 1930s as if anti-Semitism might become a substantial force in the United States, but that moment was superseded by World War II. As a whole, American anti-Semitism has been one of the least serious of all its manifestations in the Western world, at least in part because the United States has had, during the last century, phenomenal economic expansion.

The Inter-War Period. In Europe, however, the 20th century brought with it the most violent forms of anti-Semitism in all of history, worse even then the outbreaks during the Crusades or in the 17th century. The border wars in Russia and Poland in the days immediately after World War I were attended by pogroms in which many thousands were killed and hundreds of thousands were robbed and rendered homeless. The major force which perpetrated these murders was the army of the Ukrainian Democratic Republic under Simon Petliura, which made blood baths of as many as 500 places. The justification that was advanced, insofar as any rationale was offered at all, was that the Jews were supposedly partisans of the Bolsheviks. Under the impact of these horrors and the pressure mounted by the world Jewish community on the peacemakers at Versailles, minority rights for Jews, along with those for other national minorities, were written into the treaties which created such newly independent states as Poland, Lithuania, and Czechoslovakia. In the interwar period these arrangements became a source both of some protection for Jews and of considerable friction. Especially in Poland, where Jews were 10% of the population and particularly conspicuous in the cities, the essential trend between 1919 and 1939 was toward driving the Jews out of their economic positions, and toward emigration, in a world in which almost all doors were increasingly closed. The scare of Bolshevism provided the impetus for an American nativist campaign in 1921 to close the doors of the United States to further unrestricted immigration,

Wzor okladki do broszury „W szponach komunizmu".

Po Rosji i Hiszpanji — kolej na Polskę! Trzeba ją skąpać we krwi! Zostawić po niej ruiny i zgliszcza! Żyd już wiedzie kostuchę na żniwo do Polski! Baczmy na ten pochód i czuwajmy, bo gorze nam! Gorze!!!...

Nakl. „Samoobrona Narodu" Poznań   Drukarnia Centralna Poznań

Cartoon from a Polish brochure of the thirties, *In the Grip of Communism.* The Jew leads Death to his harvest in Poland, whose fate, according to the caption, will be worse than that of Russia and Spain.

especially from Eastern Europe, which meant, of course, that the doors were intentionally being closed to Jews. Even though some migration from Poland continued in this period and a relatively large number of Central European Jews did escape from Hitler after 1933, the European Jewish community as a whole had to face its destiny in Europe after World War I without the possibility of the kind of migrations which could make a radical difference. The only exception was Ereẓ Israel, where Jewish population grew from relatively negligible numbers to over half a million in this interwar period, and the foundations of the future State of Israel were laid.

GERMAN JEWRY. Up to 1932 German Jewry was in the forefront of intellectual achievement and the acquirement of free professions, though it never achieved the type of social acceptance found in other Western societies. In Germany too the development was away from the crafts and petty trade to academic professions, medium and largescale business enterprises, and public service. German Jewish society experienced during this period a certain undercurrent of tension between its acculturated strata and the *"Ostjuden,"*[29] who, whether as immigrants or as transients, caused some offense by their culture and way of life, in particular through fear of the "bad impression" they could make on cultured good Germans.

However at the end of World War I there was a rise in anti-Semitism. The defeat of Germany in war was explained by the myth, propagated by extreme right-wing elements, that circulated after 1918 of the "stab in the back" that the victorious German army had received from revolutionaries, pacifists, and intellectuals under the influence of the cowardly "Jewish spirit," as opposed to the heroic and creative "German spirit"; such accusations, combined with resentment at Jewish commercial and financial activity in Germany during the great inflation of the early 1920s there, reinforced the old stereotype evil image of the Jews. Fuel

---

[29] Ger. "Jews from the East": cognomen for Jews of East European and especially to the Jews who came from there to Germany

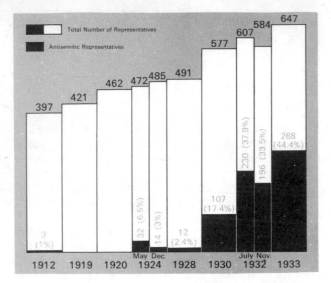

Anti-Semitic representatives in the German *Reichstag* from 1912 to 1933.

was added to the old hatred by the preeminence of Jews in many scientific fields, and, even more, their activity on the liberal and left-wing side of German politics (Walther Rathenau, minister for foreign affairs of the German republic, was assassinated in 1922; Kurt Eisner, head of the socialist republic of Bavaria in 1918, and Rosa Luxemburg, as the symbol of left-wing socialism, were murdered).

The growing influence of Adolf Hitler and the Nazis, the medieval-type poison disseminated by newspapers like *Der Stürmer,* the theories propounded by A. Rosenberg and expounded by J. Goebbels, created a dangerous situation and oppressive attitude toward Jews even before the seizure of power in Germany by Hitler in 1933. The public vote, adherence of the youth, and the growing "respectability" of the Nazis and Nazi ideas among the right wing of
German society, pointed the way to the Holocaust. The

influence of this development in the heartland of Europe, in a country and nation famous for their culture, became threatening for Jews everywhere.

Following the arrival of the Nazis to power between 1934 and 1939 all these various brands of anti-Semitism on the continent of Europe tended to merge, accepting to a greater or lesser degree the racist theory and cruel methods of the Nazis. On the other hand, this provoked growing revulsion from anti-Semitism in some conservative and Church circles, though expressed hesitatingly and not generally leading to much activity against anti-Semitism.

The Nazis set the tone in introducing racism as a basic concept in law with the Nuremberg Laws[30] (1935). They gradually tried out on European public opinion as well as "educated" German society the steps of open boycott, violence, and harsh isolation of the Jews and expropriation of their property, culminating in the *Kristallnacht*[31] action of November 9-10, 1938. The badge of a yellow *"magen David"* served to mark the Jew outwardly. Jews were given a spurious autonomy appointed by and closely supervised by specially trained "experts" of the SS and Gestapo. By the eve of World War II not only the non-communist states of Eastern Europe but also fascist Italy under Mussolini and pro-Nazi political parties in the West, like that of Oswald Mosley in England and the Croix de Feu in France, had accepted—some enthusiastically, some reluctantly—the Nazi line toward Jews, though not always all the details of Nazi behavior toward them. The civil war in Spain (1936–39), where thousands of left-wing Jews fought and died in the ranks of the international brigades of the republic against the armies of the Caudillo Franco, served in the case of the Jews, as in other aspects, to rally the

---

[30] Nazi laws excluding Jews from German citizenship, and imposing other restrictions

[31] Ger. "Night of broken glass": organized destruction of synagogues, Jewish houses and shops, accompanied by mass arrests of Jews, which took place in Germany and Austria under the Nazis on the night of Nov. 9–10, 1938

The blood libel revived in the "ritual murder number" of Julius
Streicher's Nazi newspaper *Der Stürmer*, May 1934.

extreme right wing of Europe closer to Hitler and make his
victims its enemies.

The Nazi movement succeeded in the backwash of German defeat in World War I and the creation of the Weimar

Republic and subsequent economic disaster. Jews were prominent in the very founding of Weimar and in the anti-traditional culture of the Weimar period. They were thus identified with the most "un-German" era of modern German history. This was the situation within which Nazism appealed, especially to the petty bourgeoisie who envied the seemingly ever more successful Jews, but the question of what were the ultimate roots and sources of the Nazi horrors remains a matter of controversy. The most debatable issue is whether it was a demonic aberration in which the underside of human nature broke all the bonds of civilization, or whether Nazism arose from a joining together of all of the forms of modern anti-Semitism in an outbreak armed with the most advanced technical tools of mass murder. To survey the whole history of anti-Semitism suggests that the demonic in Nazism was not so unprecedented, and that its appearance is related to a long past for which Western history cannot disclaim moral responsibility.

The Postwar Period. As a result of mass murder in World War II and of the emigration that resulted from the heightened tensions with the Arab world attending the creation of the State of Israel, Jewish residence in the classic centers of anti-Semitism, Christian Europe and the Islamic Middle East, was enormously reduced. The primary centers of Jewish population are now in the United States, the Soviet Union, and Israel. In the post-World War II era, the Jews of America rose rapidly to very close to the top of American economic, political, and intellectual life. This has been attended by remarkably few conflicts. Some social anti-Semitism does remain, for, as repeated studies have shown, the Jews are the only white group in the United States for whom social rank is consistently lower than economic status. Nonetheless, quotas in the colleges and universities and in certain professions, and exclusion from the highest posts of political life, have well-nigh ended. The visible difficulties that exist are noticeable in the Negro community. The Jew has generally been the last occupant of the neighborhoods in which Negroes now live in the large cities and Jews are therefore still quite visible as landlords and storekeepers in the Negro neighborhoods. Paradoxically, there are also resentments because Jews have been among the leading proponents of the integration of Negroes into American society and have given much of the money and the main power for these efforts. Jews are therefore often resented as being too prominent in what some Negroes would like to regard their own revolution, which other people are taking away from them in the very act of participating in it. Whatever the future may hold for anti-Semitism in America, its present temper is such that it is generally regarded as a minor problem.

The slogan "Death to the Jews" smeared on the walls of a Buenos Aires synagogue in 1961. The Hebrew inscription reads: "And thou shalt love thy neighbor as thyself."

The mood of Christians in the aftermath of World War II was overwhelmingly that of contrition. World Protestantism in its international meetings immediately after World

War II, at Amsterdam and New Delhi (1948, 1961), was at great pains to condemn anti-Semitism and to express contrition for not having acted more strongly during the Nazi era. It was in this mood, despite ongoing theological problems with the question of whether the church continues to need to convert Jews in order to be true to itself, and the further problems of understanding, from the perspective of Christian theology, the right of the Jews to the Holy Land, that there was substantial Christian support in the late 1940s, especially among Protestants, for Zionist efforts toward the creation of the State of Israel. In Catholic circles, Pius XII began the process of dissociating himself from Naziism after World War II by maintaining public neutrality during the battle for the creation of the State of Israel and insisting only on the internationalization of Jerusalem. The radical changes in Catholic-Jewish relations took place in the reign of John XXIII, with his excision of certain objectionable anti-Jewish references from the Good Friday liturgy and with his setting into motion the revision of the church's basic attitude on the Jews. This crystallized in the declaration on the subject at the Vatican Council of 1965. These revisions of attitude have made necessary further rethinking on the part of Catholics on a whole host of theological doctrines, a process of review that is still going on. A document in which the religious significance of the Holy Land for Judaism, if it be understood in its own terms, is warmly hailed, was discussed within the highest instances of the Catholic Church. There have been since the 1950s cooperative efforts between Jews and Christians of many persuasions toward the removal of anti-Semitic elements in church textbook material.

Nonetheless, the significance of the "ecumenical age" can be overestimated. Christianity is no longer the dominant spiritual power in the West that it was two centuries ago, nor has the anti-Semitism of the last modern age been primarily Christian. Therefore Christian ecumenism is less than an absolute deathblow to anti-Semitism. The increased friendship and understanding between Jews 51 and Christians has involved the most Western, modern, and intellectual elements: yet large parts of the Christian community remain unaffected. More important, in the last few years, especially since the Six-Day War of 1967 between Israel and its Arab neighbors, the Christian churches, and most especially the Protestant ones, in many places in the world, have shown evidence of an increasing hospitality to Arab anti-Israel propaganda. Much of this has emanated from the Christian churches of the Arab world. Such material has often been careful to make a distinction between anti-Semitism, which is ruled out, and anti-Zionism and opposition to Israel, which is affirmed. Nonetheless this distinction is not always maintained. In place of the old stereotype of the Jews as accursed of God for rejecting or killing Jesus, the weak and cringing figure held in contempt, a new stereotype became prevalent in some Christian circles of the Jews as arrogantly victorious and ruthless toward the Arabs.

In the aftermath of June 1967, General de Gaulle, then president of France, angered by the support the Jews of France had given to Israel, which was contrary to his political line and wishes, pronounced the Jews to be an "elitist, self-confident, and domineering people." Here and there older anti-Semitic stereotypes were used in reaction to the newest phenomena, the appearance of the Israel Jew and his effect on the Jewish mentality throughout the Diaspora. In the course of the short period of its existence, Israel has produced for the world the Jew who is unconcerned with what opinions others hold of him and who insists on his personal and national autonomy and sovereignty. This has changed the older mentalities of the majority-minority relationships to those of equality. This "new Jew" has elicited admiration, but also resentment. The newest forms of anti-Semitism have responded to the new Jewish stance by attacking what is in their eyes the elements of power. In the late 1960s considerable left-wing opinion in the world was strongly opposed to Israel and to the Jewish involvement in it. There is within this movement the paradox, but not an unprecedented one, of the presence of considerable numbers of young Jewish people who are indifferent to all forms of contemporary Jewish identity and survival.

The existence of Jews, the Jewish community, Judaism, and Jewish identity—whatever may be their self-definitions—as a people apart inevitably carries with it the prospect of that attack upon them which is termed anti-Semitism. The hatred of the unlike is an all too human phenomenon. Add to it dimensions of supposedly demonic powers; of many centuries of damnation of Jews by Christianity as the enemies of God; of the need for scapegoats in times of turmoil or defeat—and there then appears anti-Semitism, the most lasting expression in Western history of the hatred of the man who is regarded as alien, and therefore even possibly inhuman. Have that alien maintain, or have once maintained, or be believed to maintain, his own religious or cultural superiority—and thus appear to be a threat in the midst of elements of the majority—and the "great hatred" has arisen. Anti-Semitism has been less fashionable after the horror of Hitler, but it would be too hopeful to believe that its day is over.

In Arab Countries. Later Arab anti-Semitism was influenced by European anti-Semitic literature (mainly French) published in Arabic in the second half of the 19th century, particularly in connection with the Damascus Affair. In about 1869, Neophytos' *Destruction of the Jewish Religion* was published in Arabic in Beirut. In 1890 H. Fāris published in Cairo a book on the blood libel entitled *The Cry of the Innocent in the Horn of Freedom* (reissued in 1962 in the U.A.R. official series of "National Books" under the title *Talmudic Human Sacrifices*). August Rohling's *The Talmud Jew* was published in Cairo in 1899 and was cited as a source in such publications as the Arab version of the *Protocols of the of the Elders of Zion* published (c. 1967) by Shawqī 'Abd al Nāṣir, President Nasser's brother.   53

بروتوكولات
حكماء صهيون
وتعاليم التلمود

شوقي عبدالناصر

An Egyptian pamphlet called *The Protocols of the Elders of Zion* and *The Teachings of the Talmud* published by President Nasser's brother, Shawqī, 1967.

The publication of anti-Semitic literature became a spate as a result of the Arab-Israel conflict. Anti-Semitic themes and arguments were developed by Arab propaganda as a weapon against the *yishuv* during the Mandate period (1917–48) and even more so against the State of Israel. The radical objective of liquidating the Jewish state as a political entity induced Arabs to present the State of Israel as both aggressive and inherently evil, and the need to substantiate the wickedness of Israel led them to trace the sources of its evil to the history, culture, and religion of the Jewish people. Despite attempts to differentiate between Zionism and Judaism, it has been stressed repeatedly that Zionism—which is presented as a sinister, racist colonialism—originated from, and is a continuation of, Judaism. Zionism is also frequently characterized as "the executive mechanism" of Judaism. For example, H. al-Hindī and M. Ibrahim wrote in their *Isrāīl: Fikra, Ḥaraka, Dawla* ("Israel: Thought, Movement, State," Beirut, 1958, p. 113): "We fight against the imperialist regime and the Jewish people, whose invading vanguard in Palestine, called Israel, is preparing for a further leap." Though Arab anti-Semitism did not cause the Arab-Israel conflict, but rather was stimulated by it, it has aggravated Arab hostility.

The amount and vehemence of anti-Semitic literature in Arabic has no parallel in the post-World War II era. In addition to its quality and tenor, the fact that much of it has emanated from official publishing houses and government agencies makes it all the more significant, as it does not originate on the fringes of Arab society but rather at the center. The *Protocols of the Elders of Zion* has been translated into Arabic several times and been recurrently referred to, summarized, and quoted by various Arab authorities, including Nasser himself (see e.g., the official English volume of his speeches and press interviews, 1958, part 2, p. 30). Anti-Semitic themes and abstracts from the *Protocols* have been included in Arab secondary school textbooks, as e.g., in Dh. al-Hindāwī's[32] *al-Qaḍiyya a* *Falisṭīnyya* ("The Palestine Problem"), published in 1⁹

---

[32] Jordanian minister of education

danian Ministry of Education, and in indoctrina-
terial of the armed forces, as in Ḥasan Ṣabrī
...ī's [33] *Qaḍiyyat Filasṭīn* ("The Palestine Problem"),
...shed by the Indoctrination Directorate of the U.A.R.
...ed Forces. The concept of a Jewish world conspiracy,
...described in the *Protocols,* was the main theme adopted
...y Arabs from European anti-Semitism as early as the
1920s. It later may have served the psychological need of
alleviating Arab self-reproach for failures and defeats by
asserting that the Arabs fought not only against Israel, but
against "those who are behind her"—imperialism and
world Jewry.

That Arabs have not hesitated to exploit anti-Semitic
themes, despite their witnessing the moral havoc wrought
by Nazi anti-Semitism in Germany, proves the vehemence
of Arab anti-Semitism. In Arab political literature, the Nazi
extermination of the Jews has been justified. It has been
suggested that others will follow this example, and Adolf
Eichmann has been hailed as a martyr see, e.g., Abdallah
al-Tal's *Khaṭr al-Yahūdiyya Alā al-Islām wa-al-Masīhiyya*
("The Danger of World Jewry against Islam and Christianity") and M. A. 'Alūba's *Filasṭīn wa-Ḍamīr al-Insāniyya*
("Palestine and Humanity's Conscience"), both published
in Cairo in 1964. Thus, anti-Semitism has served Arab
political and intellectual leaders as a psychological tool to
prepare their people for the violent liquidation of Israel.

The quibble that the Arab anti-Jewish attitude cannot be
defined as anti-Semitism because "the Arabs themselves are
Semites" is sometimes used by Arab spokesmen, particularly in statements addressed to the outside world. Arabs have
distributed anti-Semitic literature in European languages in
various countries, and anti-Semitic groups in Europe and
America have collaborated with Arab representatives, as
the Arab states can offer them such instrumentalities as
...pport and asylum. The affiliation between Arabs and
...stern anti-Semites is manifested by the tendency of

...soldier, commander of Arab Legion in the War of Independence

post-World War II anti-Semitism to support the Arab ⌐
against Israel. Arab leaders are aware of the dilemma t
by helping to propagate anti-Semitism they may endang..
the position of the Jews in various countries and thereby
induce further Jewish migration to Israel, but their
emotions and their belief that the Arab struggle is a global
one directed against world Jewry often override other
considerations. The very meagerness of the remnants of the
Jewish communities in most Arab countries, apart from
Morocco, has been a factor limiting the development of
social anti-Semitism. However, there is clearly an element
of anti-Semitism in the persecution of Jews in Syria and
Iraq. After the Six-Day War there appeared in the Arab
press condemnations of the excessive use by Arabs of
anti-Semitic themes, specifying the damage caused by
extremism to the Arab case. The frequency of anti-Semitic
publications subsequently abated somewhat. A later book
is Bint al-Shāṭi' (Dr. 'Ā'isha 'Abd al-Raḥman),[34] A'da
al-Bashar (The Enemies of Humanity), published by the
UAR Government—The Higher Council of Islamic Affairs,
1964.

In the Soviet Bloc. THEORY AND PRACTICE. Anti-Semitism, according to Communist doctrine, is an extremely
negative social phenomenon; it could only be part of
reactionary, capitalist, and pre-capitalist regimes, in which
hatred of the Jews is exploited for the gain of the ruling
classes. Lenin, along with the other revolutionaries in
czarist Russia, was a sincere and resolute opponent of
anti-Semitism and of any form of oppression, discrimination, and persecution of Russian Jewry. However, after the
consolidation of the Soviet regime, principally under
Stalin's one-man rule, a distinctly anti-Jewish policy was
sometimes planned and implemented in the Soviet Union.
This policy consciously exploited the traditional anti-Semitism of the people in the Ukraine and in other parts of
Russia, who viewed the Jews as a foreign element, "rootless

[34] Egyptian statesman

in the homeland," who tended to conspire with the country's enemies, to evade dangerous defense duties in time of war, and who quickly profited by illicit economic manipulations and by exploiting the toiling masses. The word "Jew" itself has been mentioned relatively rarely in Soviet anti-Semitic propaganda, precisely in order to avoid breaking an ideological taboo; the anti-Semitic intent, however, was clear to everybody through the use of thinly disguised, conventional terms, as "cosmopolitans," "Zionists," "people without a fatherland," etc. The aim was mostly "educational": to produce tangible evidence that certain popular tendencies which the regime tried to eradicate (such as interest in Western life and culture, or illicit manufacturing and marketing of goods) were initiated and conducted by foreign, traitorous, "rootless" elements, i.e., the Jews. A further stimulus arose during the Cold War years, when the system of suspecting and supervising whole groups of the population by the security organs reached its peak. Every Jew was thus regarded as a real or potential security risk because of his family ties with Jews in the U.S. or other Western countries, and because of his sympathy, open or hidden, for the young State of Israel. This "cosmopolitanism," presumably an inherent characteristic of every Jewish body, was considered dangerous from the security point of view and warranted the liquidation of all Jewish institutions and organizations, with the exception of only a few synagogues which were placed under constant supervision by the security police. A further stage in Soviet anti-Semitism was reached in the late 1960s when the Soviet Union adopted an extreme anti-Israel policy, particularly after the Six-Day War in June 1967. Soviet propaganda started a campaign grotesquely inflating the image of Zionism as a sinister international conspiracy spread over the whole world, very similar to that propounded in the *Protocols of the Elders of Zion*.

AFTER THE OCTOBER REVOLUTION. During and immediately after the October Revolution, anti-Semitism served as one of the prime weapons of the Russian counterrevolution, when the White forces depicted the Bolshevik regime as executing the enslavement of Mother Russia by the Jews. Lenin saw anti-Semitism not only as a socio-political evil, in accord with his ideological outlook, but also as a formidable factor which he had to combat in his struggle for saving the revolution. He attacked anti-Semitism in his statements and speeches, including the well-known resolution of the Soviet government which defined perpetrators and instigators of pogroms as enemies of the revolution who had to be outlawed (*Izvestiya*, July 27, 1918). This atmosphere existed in the Soviet Union for years, at least up to the consolidation of Stalin's dictatorship toward the end of the 1920s. Among the masses anti-Semitic feelings continued in the 1920s, particularly during the N.E.P. ("New Economic Policy"), sometimes even increasing, as when a large influx of Jews from the townlets came to the industrial and administrative centers, where they competed for the available jobs. Anti-Semitism also increased among the peasants as Jews received land in southern Russia and Crimea for agricultural settlement. But, despite popular anti-Semitism and the official persecution of the Jewish religion and the Zionist and Jewish Socialist movement (carried out to a large extent by Jewish Communist party members), vast numbers of Jews in the U.S.S.R. enjoyed (during the 1920s and most of the 1930s) considerable geographic and social mobility, with no obstacles of an anti-Semitic nature standing in their way.

The turning point began toward the end of the 1930s with the Great Purges, during which the Soviet government discontinued denouncing and punishing expressions and outbursts of popular anti-Semitism. At this time, the government initiated a systematic liquidation of Jewish institutions and leading figures. Then, however, it was possible to view this as part of the general processes designed to secure Stalin's dictatorship, since there still were significant numbers of Jews holding middle and higher positions of power in the party hierarchy and in vital branches of government, such as the political secret police. **59**

From 1939 onward, after the signing of the Nazi-Soviet Pact (Ribbentrop-Molotov Non-Aggression Pact) and the outbreak of World War II in the West, the Soviet press and radio systematically concealed reports about the anti-Jewish character of the Nazi regime and about the oppression and murder of Jews after the invasion of Poland. In this respect, there was a considerable improvement following the German attack on the U.S.S.R. in June 1941. However, in the many detailed accounts of Nazi atrocities in the Soviet press and radio there was still a discernible tendency to cover up the fact of the genocide of the Jewish people, which was mostly described in vague terms, as the murder of "peaceful, innocent people." This systematic concealment continued even more strongly after World War II. Anyone attempting to emphasize the special suffering of the Jewish people under the Nazi occupation of the U.S.S.R. (as, e.g., Yevgeny Yevtushenko) was strongly criticized by official spokesmen.

THE BLACK YEARS 1948–1953. The Black Years began for Russian Jewry when the anti-Jewish line became the active policy of the highest government echelon. These were the last four or five years of Stalin's regime (1948–53). The secret police murdered Solomon Mikhoels, director of the Jewish State Theater in Moscow and chairman of the Jewish Anti-Fascist Committee, thus touching off what became the systematic liquidation of all Jewish cultural institutions which were remnants of the 1930s or established during the war. At the end of 1948 and the beginning of 1949 Soviet newspapers and journals opened an anti-Jewish campaign, condemning the cosmopolitan rootless elements in intellectual life. This campaign was the first undisguised expression of the wide exploitation of popular anti-Semitism for Soviet government aims. The ingrained hatred and suspicion of Jews—as a foreign element, "rootless in the soil of the homeland," liable to treason—served here as a powerful demagogic means of educating the nation against "westernizing" tendencies and for seclusion behind the wall

of Russian nationalism. The closing down of the Jewish

Anti-Fascist Committee; the arrests and execution of Jewish writers, artists, and public figures; the "Crimea Affair" trial behind closed doors; the Slansky trial in Prague (initiated and run by emissaries from the Soviet Union); the Doctors' Plot; the dismissal of many thousands of Jews from their work; and the portrayal of the State of Israel and of the Zionist movement as instruments of an anti-Soviet American spy network, were all part of the anti-Jewish program of the "Black Years." Anti-Semitism served as one of the principle tools of Stalin's regime and policy during the Cold War years both in the U.S.S.R. and in the satellite countries. According to reliable testimony, Stalin intended, following the trial of the "doctor murderers," to initiate a mass deportation of the Jewish population from the principal cities of the U.S.S.R. to Eastern Siberia, but he died in March 1953, before he could carry out his plan.

THE KHRUSHCHEV PERIOD. The period following Stalin's death was inaugurated by an apparent reversal of the anti-Jewish policy through the official retraction of the "Doctors' Plot" accusation, but expectations that the Jewish institutions would be reinstated and that there would be a vigorous campaign against popular anti-Semitism were frustrated. Nikita Khrushchev, who in a closed session of the 20th Congress of the Soviet Communist Party (February 1956) denounced Stalin and his methods, completely ignored the anti-Jewish aspect of the defunct dictator's rule, and silence on this subject was regarded as ominous for Soviet Jewry. Khrushchev himself, who was the supreme party and government representative in the Ukraine during and after World War II, was apparently deeply impressed by the immense power of popular anti-Semitism as a socio-political factor. Upon becoming prime minister and first secretary of the Communist Party of the U.S.S.R., he more than once expressed his own anti-Jewish thoughts and feelings in talks with foreign personalities, delegations, and newsmen and once even spoke out in defense of Stalin's stand in the "Crimea

Affair," thus indirectly vindicating the liquidation of the Jewish Anti-Fascist Committee and its members. Khrushchev's anti-Semitic policy was moderate in comparison with that practiced in Stalin's last years. It took the form not only of a consistent concealment of the genocide inflicted on the Jews during the Nazi invasion, but also of using Jews for show trials in the campaign against "economic crimes." This campaign was carried out by the security police from May 1961 until Khrushchev was removed from office in 1964. The Jews accused of "economic crimes" were picked out from a large number of people engaged in illicit economic activities and assigned the role of initiators, instigators, and organizers of transgressions and "crimes" against the Soviet laws in matters of production, marketing, and foreign currency regulations. Jews were the majority of those found guilty. Many of them received the death penalty, and their being Jews was emphasized in various ways in the press. During Khrushchev's office, books and pamphlets appeared which strongly denounced not only Zionism and the State of Israel, but also Judaism as such, as an extremely negative historical, cultural, and religious phenomenon. These publications were sometimes accompanied by crude anti-Semitic cartoons (as in the book by the professional Ukrainian anti-Semite Trofim Kychko, *Judaism without Embellishment,* published by the Academy of Sciences of the Ukrainian Soviet Republic, in Ukrainian, 1963). A new effort to eradicate organized Jewish life in the U.S.S.R. was made under Khrushchev through the closing of many synagogues, often following a smear campaign by the local newspapers in which the synagogues were described as hangouts where criminals met for their sinister purposes. Synagogue leaders were arrested; *minyanim* in private homes were brutally dispersed; and the baking of *mazzot* for Passover was gradually abolished. In some places, burial of Jews in separate Jewish cemeteries was discontinued. In these years, popular anti-Semitism made itself felt in several outbursts, as, e.g., the arson of the

synagogue and murder of the Jewish cemetery's *shammash*

in the town of Malakhovka near Moscow, accompanied by the posting of anti-Semitic proclamations in the streets (Rosh Ha-Shanah 1959); the burning of the synagogue in Tskhakaya, Georgia, in 1962; anti-Jewish street riots, at times incited by blood libels (in Tashkent and in Tskhaltubo in 1962); public tension created by a blood-libel story in Vilna in 1963; and in one instance, the publication of an anti-Jewish blood libel in the official organ of the Communist Party (in the town Buinaksk, Dagestan, in the local newspaper on Aug. 9, 1961, where a few days later an official apology of sorts was printed). In widespread circles of the Russian intelligentsia opposition to the official and popular anti-Semitic clime was expressed in several ways, but for the most part by hints and implications rather than by overt criticism. It reached its climax in Yevtushenko's poem *Babi Yar* published in *Literaturnaya Gazeta* in 1961 and in the fact that Dmitri Shostakovich included the poem in one of the movements of his 13th symphony. The poem immediately aroused severe criticism, with anti-Semitic overtones, on the part of official literary critics and even from Khrushchev himself. A clear hint was given that any public declaration on behalf of the Jews was in contradiction to official policy. At the same time Jews of the U.S.S.R. were affected by systematic discrimination in many spheres. Jews almost completely disappeared from the foreign service, from commanding posts in the army, from positions as representatives of the government, the party hierarchy, the judiciary, etc. The number of Jews in local, republican, or Soviet government bodies fell far below the percentage of Jews, not only in the cities (where about 95% of the Jews reside), but in the population as a whole. Young Jews met with increasing difficulties in getting accepted in higher institutions of learning in the main cities of Russia and the Ukraine, particularly in those fields of study which usually lead to positions of power or to classified fields.

UNDER KOSIGIN-BREZHNEV. When Khrushchev was demoted in October 1964, and the "collective leadership" headed by Alexei Kosigin and Leonid Brezhnev initiated, 63

Dayan to Hitler: Move on!

Kazakhstanskaya Pravda, June 21, 1967.

there were signs of slight improvement in the attitude to Soviet Jewry. The campaign against "economic crimes" and the synagogues ceased; baking of *mazzot* was to a certain extent renewed; Jews were mentioned as victims of the Nazi Holocaust on Soviet soil; and even a public denunciation of anti-Semitism as one of the evils of society

Sovietskaya Rossia
July 1, 1967
Moscow

In step.

was once made in a speech by Prime Minister Kosigin. Following this, editorials in the same spirit were published in several leading newspapers in 1965. However, after the Six-Day War in June 1967 between Israel and the Arab states, a most severe anti-Jewish campaign in the Soviet press and propaganda media was unleashed again. Its declared aim was to condemn Israel and Zionism, but its general spirit and the caricatures accompanying it were markedly anti-Semitic. The Ukrainian style of anti-Semitism, which represents Judaism as a criminal religious tradition from ancient times, educating its followers in racial superiority and hatred of other peoples, began reappearing in widely diffused publications, as well as in tracts written by Trofim Kychko who reappeared on the scene after having had to remain silent for a few years, as his 1963 book had caused a world-wide scandal even in Communist parties in the West. In the new campaign, "Zionism" was assigned a central place: it was depicted as a powerful instrument or a main ally of "imperialism," serving its sinister global aims, such as enslaving nations and exploiting them, undermining Socialism, and, of course, manipulating Israel for criminal aggression against the progressive Arab states. These descriptions of Zionism closely resembled the description of the world Jewish conspiracy in the *Protocols of the Elders of Zion.* It created an atmosphere of depression and deep apprehension in Soviet Jewry, who again were led to fear for their physical and economic security. However, no persecutions of Jews in the manner of the "Black Years" of Stalin are known to have taken place; it seems that the government took steps to prevent any outbursts of popular anti-Semitism such as those which occurred in Khrushchev's time.

POLAND AND CZECHOSLOVAKIA. Popular expression of anti-Semitism in Poland became overt once more when Gomulka's government rose to power in October 1956. One of its sources was hatred of the overthrown Stalinist higher echelon, which in Poland included a number of Jews in key positions (e.g., Jacob Berman and Hilary Minc). However, Gomulka's regime was expressly opposed to anti-Semitism. In the framework of repatriation of former Polish citizens, it made possible the return of many Jews from the U.S.S.R. and their further migration to Israel. It did not interfere with the exodus of the remnant of Polish Jewry to Israel and other countries. However, its policy underwent a marked change following the Six-Day War in June 1967, becoming extremely anti-Israel, in line with Soviet policy. Gomulka even went a step further, when he publicly warned the Jews in Poland against becoming a "fifth column" by expressions of sympathy for Israel. Following this stand, a number of books and articles appeared that sharply attacked Israel and Zionism, with distinctly anti-Semitic overtones. This paved the way for wide anti-Jewish purges in the ranks of the government, universities, and other fields in the spring of 1968, when government circles blamed "Zionists" for mass demonstrations held by students and professors in the universities. The anti-Jewish purge and propaganda campaign was directed and exploited by one of the party factions for political ends. This faction, known as the "Partisans," was headed by the minister of the interior and head of the security police, Mieczysław Moczar.

In Czechoslovakia, where traditional anti-Semitism has no deep roots, as in the Ukraine and in Poland, Antonin Novotny, president of the republic and secretary of the Communist Party, ruled continuously from the period of the Slansky Trial until early in 1968. When he was ousted by the liberal wing of the Communist Party, there was a general improvement in the atmosphere. Jewish cultural and religious life was favorably affected. But, during the sharp controversy between the Soviet government and the liberal regime in Prague that led to the invasion of Czechoslovakia by the Soviet army in August 1968, Soviet and Polish propaganda used anti-Jewish allusions (e.g., that "Zionists" had pulled the strings of the "counterrevolution" in Czechoslovakia). Following the invasion, Jewish figures in the liberal Czechoslovak regime, such as Eduard Goldstuecker, Ota Šik, and others, were forced to disappear or even to leave the country. In the Czechoslovak crisis, as in the anti-Jewish purges in Poland that year, anti-Semitism, mostly disguised as "anti-Zionism," was one of the prime elements in the influence exerted by Soviet agencies in Soviet bloc countries; it naturally served even more the needs of the anti-Israel campaign conducted by the Soviet government and propaganda media in Arab countries.

2 BLOOD LIBEL

The notorious allegation that Jews murder non-Jews, especially Christians, in order to obtain blood for the Passover or other rituals is a complex of deliberate lies, trumped-up accusations, and popular beliefs about the murder-lust of the Jews and their bloodthirstiness, based on the conception that Jews hate Christianity and mankind in general. It is combined with the delusion that Jews are in some way not human and must have recourse to special remedies and subterfuges in order to appear, at least outwardly, like other men. The blood libel led to trials and massacres of Jews in the Middle Ages and early modern times; it was revived by the Nazis. Its origin is rooted in ancient, almost primordial, concepts concerning the potency and energies of blood.

Origins. Blood sacrifices were practiced by many pagan religions. They are expressly forbidden by the Torah. The law of meat-salting *(melihah)* is designed to prevent the least drop of avoidable blood remaining in food. Yet pagan incomprehension of the Jewish monotheist cult, lacking the customary images and statues, led to charges of ritual killing. At a time of tension between Hellenism and Judaism, it was alleged that the Jews would kidnap a Greek foreigner, fatten him up for a year, and then convey him to a wood, where they slew him, sacrificed his body with the customary ritual, partook of his flesh, and while immolating the Greek swore an oath of hostility to the Greeks. This was told, according to Apion, to King Antiochus Epiphanes by an intended Greek victim who had been found in the Jewish Temple being fattened by the Jews for this sacrifice and was saved by the king (Jos.,

Apion, 2:89–102). Some suspect that stories like this were spread intentionally as propaganda for Antiochus Epiphanes to justify his profanation of the Temple. Whatever the immediate cause, the tale is the outcome of hatred of the Jews and incomprehension of their religion.

To be victims of this accusation was also the fate of other misunderstood religious minorities. In the second century C.E. the Church Father Tertullian complained: "We are said to be the most criminal of men, on the score of our sacramental baby-killing, and the baby-eating that goes with it." He complains that judicial torture was applied to Christians because of this accusation, for "it ought . . . to be wrung out of us [whenever that false charge is made] how many murdered babies each of us has tasted . . . Oh! the glory of that magistrate who had brought to light some Christian who had eaten up to date a hundred babies!" (*Apologeticus,* 7:1 and 1:12, Loeb edition (1931), 8, 36).

Middle Ages. During the Middle Ages some heretical Christian sects were afflicted by similar accusations. The general attitude of Christians toward the holy bread of the Communion created an emotional atmosphere in which it was felt that the divine child was mysteriously hidden in the partaken bread. The popular preacher, Friar Berthold of Regensburg (13th century), felt obliged to explain why communicants do not actually see the holy child by asking the rhetorical question, "Who would like to bite off a baby's head or hand or foot?" Popular beliefs and imaginings of the time, either of classical origin or rooted in Germanic superstitions, held that blood, even the blood of executed malefactors or from corpses, possesses the property of healing or causing injury. Thus, combined with the general hatred of Jews then prevailing, a charge of clandestine cruel practices and blood-hunting, which had evolved among the pagans and was used against the Christians, was deflected by Christian society to the most visible and persistent minority in opposition to its tenets.

As Christianity spread in Western Europe and penetrated the popular consciousness, influencing the 69 emotions and imagination even more than thought and dogma, various story elements began to evolve around the alleged inhumanity and sadism of the Jews. In the first distinct case of blood libel against Jews in the Middle Ages, that of Norwich in 1144, it was alleged that the Jews had "bought a Christian child [the 'boy-martyr' William] before Easter and tortured him with all the tortures wherewith our Lord was tortured, and on Long Friday hanged him on a rood in hatred of our Lord." The motif of torture and murder of Christian children in imitation of Jesus' Passion persisted with slight variations throughout the 12th century (Gloucester, England, 1168; Blois, France, 1171; Saragossa, Spain, 1182), and was repeated in many libels of the 13th century. In the case of Little Saint Hugh of Lincoln, 1255, it would seem that an element taken directly from Apion's libel (see above) was interwoven into the Passion motif, for the chronicler Matthew Paris relates, "that the Child was first fattened for ten days with white bread and milk and then . . . almost all the Jews of England were invited to the crucifixion." The crucifixion motif was generalized in the *Siete Partidas* law code of Spain, 1263: "We have heard it said that in certain places on Good Friday the Jews do steal children and set them on the cross in a mocking manner." Even when other motifs eventually predominated in the libel, the crucifixion motif did not disappear altogether. On the eve of the expulsion of the Jews from Spain, there occurred the blood-libel case of "the Holy Child of La Guardia" (1490–91). There, Conversos were made to confess under torture that with the knowledge of the chief rabbi of the Jews they had assembled in a cave, crucified the child, and abused him and cursed him to his face, as was done to Jesus in ancient times. The crucifixion motif explains why the blood libels occurred at the time of Passover.

The Jews were well aware of the implications of sheer sadism involved in the libel. In a dirge lamenting the Jews massacred at Munich because of a blood libel in 1286, the anonymous poet supposedly quotes the words of the

St
Hugo's Tomb
*as it stands in Dr Stukeleys
Itinerar.*

Alleged tomb of Hugh of Lincoln. From D. Tovey's *Anglia Judaica*, Oxford, 1738. Cecil Roth Collection.

Christian killers: "These unhappy Jews are sinning, they kill Christian children, they torture them in all their limbs, they take the blood cruelly to drink" (A. M. Habermann (ed.), *Sefer Gezerot Ashkenaz ve-Zarefat* (1946), 199). This ironical "quotation" contains an added motif in the libels, the thirst of the Jew for blood, out of his hatred for the good and true. This is combined in 13th-century Germany with the conception that the Jew cannot endure purity: he hates the innocence of the Christian child, its joyous song and appearance. This motif, found in the legendary tales of the monk Caesarius of Heisterbach in Germany, underwent various transmutations. In the source from which Caesarius took his story the child killed by the Jews sings *erubescat judaeus* ("let the Jew be shamed"). In Caesarius' version, the child sings the *Salve Regina.* The Jews cannot endure this pure laudatory song and try to frighten him and stop him from singing it. When he refuses they cut off his tongue and hack him to pieces. About a century after the expulsion of the Jews from England the cultural motif only became the basis of Geoffrey Chaucer's "Prioress' Tale." Here the widow's little child sings the *Alma Redemptoris Mater* while "the serpent Sathanas, That hath in Jews herte his waspes nest" awakens indignation in the cruel Jewish heart: "O Hebraik peple, allas! /Is this to yow a thing that is honest,/That swich a boy shal waeken as him lest/In your despyt, and singe of swich sentence / Which is agayn your lawes reverence?" The Jews obey the promptings of their Satanic master and kill the child; a miracle brings about their deserved punishment. Though the scene of this tale is laid in Asia, at the end of the story Chaucer takes care to connect Asia explicitly with bygone libels in England, and the motif of hatred of the innocent with the motif of mockery of the crucifixion: "O yonge Hugh of Lincoln, slayn also / With cursed Jewes, as it is notable, / For it nis but a litel whyle ago ; / Preye eek for us."

In the blood libel of Fulda (1235) another motif comes to the fore: the Jews taking blood for medicinal remedies (here of five young Christian boys). The strange medley of ideas about the use of blood by the Jews is summed up by the end of the Middle Ages, in 1494, by the citizens of Tyrnau (Trnava). The Jews need blood because "firstly, they were convinced by the judgment of their ancestors, that the blood of a Christian was a good remedy for the alleviation of the wound of circumcision. Secondly, they were of opinion that this blood, put into food, is very efficacious for the awakening of mutual love. Thirdly, they had discovered, as men and women among them suffered equally from menstruation, that the blood of a Christian is a specific medicine for it, when drunk. Fourthly, they had an ancient but secret ordinance by which they are under obligation to shed Christian blood in honor of God, in daily sacrifices, in some spot or other . . . the lot for the present year had fallen on the Tyrnau Jews." To the motifs of crucifixion, sadism, hatred of the innocent and of Christianity, and the unnaturalness of the Jews and its cure by the use of good Christian blood, there were added, from time to time, the ingredients of sorcery, perversity, and a kind of "blind obedience to a cruel tradition." Generation after generation of Jews in Europe was tortured, and Jewish communities were massacred or dispersed and broken up because of the blood libel. It was spread by various agents. Popular preachers ingrained it in the minds of the common people. It became embedded, through miracle tales, in their imagination and beliefs. This caused in Moravia, in about 1343, "a woman of ill fame to come with the help of another woman and propose to an old Jew of Brno, named Osel, her child for sale for six marks, because the child was red in hair and in face. The Jew simulated gladness, immediately gave three marks to the woman, and invited them to come with the child to a cellar the next day, early in the morning, under the pretext that he had to consult about the buying of the child with the bishop of the Jews and the elders." The Jew invited Christian officials, who imprisoned the women and punished them horribly (B. Bretholz, *Quellen zur Geschichte der Juden in Maehren* (1935), 27–28).

The majority of the heads of state and the church opposed the circulation of the libel. Emperor Frederick II of Hohenstaufen decided, after the Fulda libel, to clear up the matter definitively, and have all the Jews in the empire killed if the accusation proved to be true, or exonerate them publicly if false, using this as an occasion to arbitrate in a matter affecting the whole of Christendom. The enquiry into the blood libel was thus turned into an all-Christian problem. The emperor, who first consulted the recognized church authorities, later had to turn to a device of his own. In the words of his summing-up of the enquiry in which it was found that the usual church authorities "expressed various opinions about the case, and as they have been proved incapable of coming to a conclusive decision . . . we found it necessary . . . to turn to such people that were once Jews and have converted to the worship of the Christian faith; for they, as opponents, will not be silent about anything that they may know in this matter against the Jews." The emperor adds that he himself was already convinced, through his knowledge and wisdom, that the Jews were innocent. He sent to the kings of the West, asking them to send him decent and learned converts to Christianity to consult in the matter. The synod of converts took place and came to the conclusion, which the emperor published: "There is not to be found, either in the Old or the New Testament, that the Jews are desirous of human blood. On the contrary, they avoid contamination with any kind of blood." The document quotes from various Jewish texts in support, adding, "There is also a strong likelihood that those to whom even the blood of permitted animals is forbidden, cannot have a hankering after human blood. Against this accusation stand its cruelty, its unnaturalness, and the sound human emotions which the Jews have also in relation to the Christians. It is also unlikely that they would risk [through such a dangerous action] their life and property." A few years later, in 1247, Pope Innocent IV wrote that "Christians charge falsely . . . that [the Jews] hold a communion rite . . . with the heart of a murdered child; and should the cadaver of a dead man happen to be found anywhere they maliciously lay it to their charge." Neither emperor nor pope were heeded.

Jewish scholars in the Middle Ages bitterly rejected this inhuman accusation. They quoted the Law and instanced the Jewish way of life in order to refute it. The general opinion of the Jews is summed up thus: "You are libeling us for you want to find a reason to permit the shedding of our blood." However, the Jewish denial of these accusations like the opinion of enlightened Christian leaders, did not succeed in preventing the blood libels from shaping to a large extent the image of the Jew transmitted from the

A 15th-century German woodcut showing Jews extracting blood from Simon of Trent, subject of the Italian blood libel of 1475.

Middle Ages to modern times. (It was only in 1965 that the church officially repudiated the blood libel of Trent by cancelling the beatification of Simon and the celebrations in his honor.)

Modern Times. From the 17th century, blood-libel cases increasingly spread to Eastern Europe (Poland-Lithuania). The atmosphere at such trials is conveyed by the protocols of the investigation of two Jews and a Jewess who were put to torture in a blood-libel case at Lublin in 1636: "The Jew Baruch answers: 'I haven't seen the child.' Second torture: 'I am innocent and other Jews are innocent.' Third torture: 'I am innocent and other Jews are innocent, and everything that Joseph [the accuser] said is a lie. Jews need no Christian blood.'" Fegele the Jewess struggled courageously to defend the truth, as evident in the cross-examination: "Judge: 'Are you acquainted with sorcery?' Fegele: 'I never dabble in this. I am a poor widow who sells vodka and *kwas*'; Judge: 'For what purpose do Jews need Christian blood?' Fegele: 'Jews need no Christian blood, either of adults or of children'; Judge: 'Where have you hidden the child's blood?' Fegele: 'The use of blood is forbidden to Jews, even of animal blood'; Judge: 'For what purpose do Jews need Christian blood?' Fegele: 'Jews use no Christian blood.' Judge: 'And are you a sorceress?' Fegele: 'No. I have nothing to do with this.'" She remained unbroken under torture, and even the threat of torture with a red-hot iron. Hugo Grotius, the Protestant legal philosopher, when told about the case expressed the opinion that the blood accusation was simply a libel generated by hatred of the Jews, and recalled that the early Christians and later Christian sectarians were accused in a similar way (Balaban, in *Festschrift S. Dubnow* (1930), 87–112).

In Eastern Europe, as late as the 17th century, the blood libel is identified with Jewish sorcery in the minds of the accusers, while the motif of the use of Christian blood for Passover *mazzot* increasingly comes to the fore. As conditions in Poland deteriorated, blood-libel cases multiplied. Through the Councils of the Lands[35] the Jews sent an emissary to the Holy See who succeeded in having an investigation ordered and carried out by Cardinal Lorenzo Ganganelli, later Pope Clement XIV. In a detailed report submitted in 1759 Ganganelli examined the veracity of the blood libel in general and of the recent cases in Poland-Lithuania in particular, quoting *in extenso* from former church authorities against the libel. His main conclusion was: "It may be realized with what lively faith we ought to ask God with the Psalmist, 'deliver me from the calumnies of men.' For it cannot be denied that 'Calumny maketh the wise man mad and destroyeth the strength of his heart.' . . . I therefore hope that the Holy See will take some measure to protect the Jews of Poland as Saint Bernard, Gregory IX, and Innocent IV did for the Jews of Germany and France, 'that the name of Christ be not blasphemed' by the Jews."

In the 19th century the ringleaders of Jew-hatred in its modern form of anti-Semitism made conspicuous use of the blood libel for incitement against Jews in various countries. It was also used as a weapon to arouse the uneducated masses for specific political reasons, as occurred, for instance, in the Damascus Affair (1840) in the struggle among the western powers for influence in the Near East. Anti-Semitic "experts" wrote treatises which set out to prove the truth of the libel from the records of past accusations and Jewish sources. Two such were Konstantin Cholewa de Pawlikowski (*Talmud in der Theorie und Praxis,* Regensburg, 1866) and H. Desportes (*Le mystère du sang chez les Juifs de tous les temps,* Paris, 1859, with a preface by the notorious anti-Semite E. Drumont). In the blood-libel trials held in the second half of the 19th and early 20th century, such as the Tiszaeszlar and Beilis cases, "experts" such as August Rohling appeared to testify in court; all were irrefutably answered by Jewish and pro-Jewish scholars (J.S. Bloch, H.L. Strack, J. Mazeh).

[35] Central institutions of Jewish self-government in Poland and Lithuania from the middle of the 16th cent. until 1764

Another weapon developed in the arsenal of anti-Semitism was an insidious way of implying the truth of the blood-libel charge by stating it as a fact without denying it. A notorious example is found in the article *Blut* (in *Handwoerterbuch des deutschen Aberglaubens,* 1 (1927), cols. 1434–42) where it is remarked (col. 1436): *"Moses verbot umsonst das Bluttrinken"* ("Moses in vain prohibited the drinking of blood"), and *"Dass die Frage der juedischen Ritualmorde immer noch nicht verschwunden ist, lehren Prozesse neuerer Zeit"* ("Trials in modern times show the problem of ritual murder has still not disappeared"; col. 1439).

The Nazis unashamedly used the blood libel in full force for anti-Jewish propaganda. They revived old allegations and instituted reinvestigations and trials in territories under their rule or influence: at Memel in 1936; at Bamberg in 1937 (a revival); and at Velhartice, Bohemia, in 1940. On May 1, 1934, the Nazi daily, *Der Stuermer,* devoted a special horrifyingly illustrated number to the blood libel, in which German scientists openly served the Nazi aims. The above-mentioned *Handwoerterbuch* (vol. 7 (1935–36), cols. 727–39) printed an article entitled *Ritualmord* written by Peuckert, a man who remained active and respected in German science, which is throughout simply an affirmation and propagation of the blood libel, although using some cautious phrasing. The epitome appears in the remarkable enquiry: *"Es mag im Anschluss an dieses erschuetternde Register nur noch die Frage behandelt werden: zu welchem Zweck verwendeten die Juden das Blut?"* ("In conclusion to this shocking list, there remains only one question: for what purpose did the Jews use the blood?"; col. 734).

The blood libel, in the various forms it assumed and the tales with which it was associated, is one of the most terrible expressions of the combination of human cruelty and credulity. No psychological or sociological research can convey the depths to which the numerous intentional instigators of such libels, and the more numerous propagators of this phantasmagoria, sank. It resulted in the torture, murder, and expulsion, of countless Jews, and the misery of insults. However, the dark specters it raised were even more harmful in their effects on the minds of Christians. The Jew had only to refer to himself, his upbringing, laws, way of life, and attitude to other people and to cruelty, to perceive the falsity and baselessness of these allegations. In modern times Aḥad Ha-Am[36] found "some consolation" in the existence of the blood libel, for it could serve as a spiritual defense against the influence on Jewish self-evaluation of the consensus of hostile opinion. "This accusation is the solitary case in which the general acceptance of an idea about ourselves does not make us doubt whether all the world can be wrong, and we right, because it is based on an absolute lie, and is not even supported by any false inference from particular to universal. Every Jew who has been brought up among Jews knows as an indisputable fact that throughout the length and breadth of Jewry there is not a single individual who drinks human blood for religious purposes. . . . Let the world say what it will about our moral inferiority: we know that its ideas rest on popular logic, and have no real scientific basis. . . . 'But'—you ask—'is it possible that everybody can be wrong, and the Jews right?' Yes, it is possible: the blood accusation proves it possible. Here, you see, the Jews are right and perfectly innocent" (*Selected Essays* (1962), 203–4).

IN RUSSIA. In modern times Russia has been the principal perpetuator of the blood libel, both medieval and modern factors (see above) combining to enable its deliberate dissemination among the ignorant masses. The first blood-libel case in Russia occurred in the vicinity of Senno, south of Vitebsk, on the eve of Passover 1799, when the body of a woman was found near a Jewish tavern: four Jews were arrested on the ground of the "popular belief that the Jews require Christian blood." Apostates supplied the court with extracts from a distorted translation of the

Shulḥan Arukh [37] and *Shevet Yehudah*. [38] The accused were released through lack of evidence. Nevertheless the poet and administrator G.R. Derzhavin, in his "Opinion submitted to the czar on the organization of the status of the Jews in Russia," could state that "in these communities persons are to be found who perpetrate the crime, or at least afford protection to those committing the crime, of shedding Christian blood, of which Jews have been suspected at various times and in different countries. If I for my part consider that such crimes, even if sometimes committed in antiquity, were carried out by ignorant fanatics, I thought it right not to overlook them." Thus a semiofficial and "highbrow" seal was given to the libel in Russia at the opening of the 19th century. Official Russian circles were divided in their views on the libel. A number of inquiries into the charges were instituted, while the views of the czars themselves fluctuated; the emperors and popes of the Middle Ages (see above) can be pointed to as models of enlightenment in comparison with the rulers of czarist Russia.

Between 1805 and 1816 various cases of blood libel occurred in places within the Pale of Settlement, [39] and the investigations always ended by exposing the lie on which they were based. In an attempt to stop their dissemination the minister of ecclesiastic affairs, A. Golitsyn, sent a circular to the heads of the governments (provinces) throughout Russia on March 6, 1817, to this effect. Basing his instruction on the fact that both the Polish monarchs and the popes have invariably invalidated the libels, and that they had been frequently refuted by judicial inquiries, he stated in his circular that the czar directed "that henceforward the Jews shall not be charged with murdering Christian children, without evidence, and through prejudice alone that they allegedly require Christian blood."

[37] Joseph Caro's code of Jewish Law (1564-5)
[38] Solomon ibn Verga's historical book (c. 1520)
[39] 25 provinces of Czarist Russia where Jews were permitted permanent residence

Nevertheless Alexander I (1801–25) gave instructions to revive the inquiry in the case of the murder of a Christian child in Velizh (near Vitebsk) where the assassins had not been found and local Jewish notables had been blamed for the crime. The trial lasted for about ten years. Although the Jews were finally exonerated, Nicholas I later refused to endorse the 1817 circular, giving as a reason that he considered that "there are among the Jews savage fanatics or sects requiring Christian blood for their ritual, and especially since to our sorrow such fearful and astonishing groups also exist among us Christians." Other blood libels occurred in Telsiai (Telz) in the government (province) of Kovno, in 1827, and Zaslav (Izyaslav), in the government of Volhynia, in 1830. The Hebrew writer and scholar I. B. Levinsohn was stirred by this case to write his book *Efes Damim* (Vilna, 1837), in which he exposed the senselessness of the accusations. A special secret commission was convened by the Russian Ministry of Foreign Affairs to clarify the problem concerning "use by Jews of the blood of Christian children," in which the Russian lexicographer and folklorist V. Dahl took part. The result of the inquiry, which reviewed numerous cases of blood libel in the Middle Ages and modern period, were published in 1844 in a limited edition and presented by Skripitsin, the director of the Department for Alien Religions, to the heads of state. In 1853, a blood libel occurred in Saratov, when two Jews and an apostate were found guilty of the murder of two Christian children—the only instance in Russia of its kind. The council of state which dealt with the case in its final stages announced that it had confined itself to the purely legal aspect of the case and refrained from "anything bearing on the secret precepts or sects existing within Judaism and their influence on the crime." It thereby *prima facie* deprived the case of its test character as a blood libel. While the case was being considered, between 1853 and 1860, various Jews were accused of "kidnapping" on a number of occasions. The special committee appointed in 1855 had included a number of theologians and orientalists, 81 among them two converts from Judaism, V. Levisohn and D. Chwolson. The committee reviewed numerous Hebrew publications and manuscripts, and came to the conclusion that there was no hint or evidence to indicate that the Jews made use of Christian blood.

With the growth of an anti-Semitic movement in Russia in the 1870s, the blood libel became a regular motif in the anti-Jewish propaganda campaign conducted in the press and literature. Leading writers in this sphere were H. Lutostansky, who wrote a pamphlet "concerning the use of Christian blood by Jewish sects for religious purposes" (1876), which ran into many editions, and J. Pranaitis. Numerous further allegations were made, including a case in Kutais (Georgia) in 1879, in which Jewish villagers were accused of murdering a little Christian girl. The case was tried in the district court and gave the advocates for the defense an opportunity of ventilating the social implications of the affair and the malicious intentions of its instigators. The chief agitators of the blood libels were monks. At the monastery of Suprasl crowds assembled to gaze on the bones of the "child martyr Gabriello," who had been allegedly murdered by Jews in 1690. The wave of blood libels which occurred at the end of the 19th century in central Europe, including the cases in Tiszaeszlar in 1881, Xanten in 1891, Polna in 1899, etc., also heaped fuel on the flames of the agitation in Russia.

A number of works were published by Jewish writers in Russia to contradict the allegations, such as D. Chwolson's "Concerning Medieval Libels against Jews" (1861); I. B. Levinsohn's *Efes Damim* was translated into Russian (1883). Some of the calumniators were also prosecuted, such as Hyppolite Lutostanski in 1880. Despite the growing anti-Semitism and its officially supported anti-Jewish policy, the czarist authorities during the reign of Alexander III (1881–94) did not lend credence to the blood libels. It was only at the beginning of the 20th century that further attempts were renewed. These included the Blondes Case in Vilna, in 1900, and an attempt in Dubossary, in the government of Kherson, where a Russian criminal tried to pin the murder of a child on the Jews. However, with the victory of the reactionaries in Russia after the dissolution of the Second Duma[40] in 1907, and the strengthening of the extreme right wing (Union of Russian People) in the Third Duma, another attempt at official level was made by the regime to use the blood libel as a weapon in its struggle against the revolutionary movement and to justify its policy toward the Jews. An opportunity for doing so occurred in the Beilis Case engineered by the minister of justice Shcheglovitov. The trial, which continued from spring 1911 to fall 1913, became a major political issue and the focal point for anti-Jewish agitation in the anti-Semitic press, in the streets, at meetings, and in the Duma. The whole of liberal and socialist opinion was ranged behind Beilis' defense, and even a section of the conservative camp. Leading Russian lawyers conducted the defense, and in Russia and throughout Europe hundreds of intellectuals and scholars, headed by V. Korolenko and M. Gorki, joined in protest against the trial. The exoneration of Beilis was a political defeat for the regime. Despite this, the government continued to assent to the instigation of blood libels and support their dissemination among the masses until the 1917 Revolution. The Soviet government's attitude toward the blood libel was that it had been a weapon of the reaction and a tactic to exploit popular superstition by the czarist regime. The instigators of the Beilis trial were interrogated and tried at an early stage after the revolution. In later years the specter of the blood libel has been raised in the Soviet press in remote regions of the U.S.S.R., such as Georgia, Dagestan, and Uzbekistan, in the context of the violent propaganda campaign conducted by the Soviet government against Judaism and the State of Israel. After these attempts had aroused world public opinion, they were dropped.

[40] Imperial Russian legislature, between 1906 and 1917

3 JEWISH BADGE

Muslim World. The introduction of a mark to distinguish persons not belonging to the religious faith of the majority did not originate in Christendom, where it was later radically imposed, but in Islam. It seems that Caliph Omar II (717–20), not Omar I, as is sometimes stated, was the first ruler to order that every non-Muslim, the *dhimmī,* should wear vestimentary distinctions (called *giyār,* i.e., distinguishing marks) of a different color for each minority group. The ordinance was unequally observed, but it was reissued and reinforced by Caliph al-Mutawakkil (847–61). Subsequently it remained in force over the centuries, with a few variations.

Christendom. Although written documentary testimony concerning distinctive signs worn by Jews from the 12th century is still lacking, pictorial representations of this period, especially in the Germanic countries, introduce the pointed hat. This is subsequently referred to as the "Jewish hat," worn by Jews or depicted in allegorical representations of Judaism ("Synagoga"). It would seem, however, that this distinction was instituted by the Jews themselves. There are some ambiguous references to the compulsory imposition of distinctive Jewish clothing in documents from the beginning of the 13th century (Charter of Alais, 1200: Synodal rules of Odo, bishop of Paris, c. 1200). The consistent record, however, can be traced back only to canon 68 of the Fourth Lateran Council (1215): "In several provinces, a difference in vestment distinguishes the Jews or the Saracens from the Christians; but in others, the confusion has reached such proportions that a difference can no longer be perceived. Hence, at times it has occurred that Christians have had sexual intercourse in error with Jewish or Saracen women and Jews or Saracens with Christian women. That the crime of such a sinful mixture shall no longer find evasion or cover under the pretext of error, we order that they [Jews and Saracens] of both sexes, in all Christian lands and at all times, shall be publicly differentiated from the rest of the population by the quality of their garment, especially since that this is ordained by Moses. . . ." Both the allusion to biblical law (Lev. 19), and the inclusion of the canon among a series of others regulating the Jewish position, indicate that the decree was directed especially against the Jews.

Implementation of the council's decision varied in the countries of the West in both the form of the distinctive sign and the date of its application.

ENGLAND. In England papal influence was at this time particularly strong. The recommendations of the Lateran Council were repeated in an order of March 30, 1218. However, before long the wealthier Jews, and later on entire communities, paid to be exempted, notwithstanding the reiteration of the order by the diocesan council of Oxford in 1222. In 1253, however, the obligation to wear the badge was renewed in the period of general reaction, by Henry III, who ordered the *tabula* to be worn in a prominent position. In the *statutum de Judeismo* of 1275, Edward I stipulated the color of the badge and increased the size. A piece of yellow taffeta, six fingers long and three broad, was to be worn above the heart by every Jew over the age of seven years. In England, the badge took the form of the Tablets of the Law, considered to symbolize the Old Testament, in which form it is to be seen in various caricatures and portraits of medieval English Jews.

FRANCE. In 1217, the papal legate in southern France ordered that the Jews should wear a *rota* ("wheel") on their outer garment but shortly afterward the order was rescinded. However, in 1219 King Philip Augustus ordered the Jews to wear the badge, apparently in the same form. Discussions regarding the permissibility of wearing the

A red and white circular badge worn by French Jews in the 13th and 14th centuries. A drawing after a French 14th-century miniature. Paris, Bibliothèque Nationale, ms. Francais 820, fol. 192.

badge on the Sabbath when not attached to the garment are reported by Isaac b. Moses of Vienna, author of the *Or Zaru'a,* who was in France about 1217–18. Numerous church councils (Narbonne 1227, Rouen 1231, Arles 1234, Béziers 1246, Albi 1254, etc.) reiterated the instructions for wearing the badge, and a general edict for the whole of France was issued by Louis IX (Saint Louis) on June 19, 1269. This edict was endorsed by Philip the Bold, Philip the Fair, Louis X, Philip V, and others, and by the councils of Pont-Audemer (1279), Nîmes (1284), etc. The circular badge was normally to be worn on the breast; some regulations also required that a second sign should be worn on the back. At times, it was placed on the bonnet or at the level of the belt. The badge was yellow in color, or of two shades, white and red. Wearing it was compulsory from the age of either seven or thirteen years. Any Jew found without the badge forfeited his garment to his denunciator. In cases of a second offense a severe fine was imposed. When traveling, the Jew was exempted from wearing the badge. Philip the Fair extracted fiscal benefits from the compulsory wearing of the badge, by annual distribution of the badges by the royal tax collectors at a fixed price.

SPAIN. The obligation to wear the Badge of Shame was reenacted by the secular authorities in Spain shortly after the promulgation of the decrees of the Lateran Council, and in 1218 Pope Honorius III instructed the archbishop of Toledo to see that it was rigorously enforced. The Spanish Jews did not submit to this passively, and some of them threatened to leave the country for the area under Muslim rule. In consequence, the pope authorized the enforcement of the regulation to be suspended. The obligation was indeed reenacted sporadically (e.g., in Aragon 1228, Navarre 1234, Portugal 1325). However, it was not consistently enforced, and Jews who had influence at court would often secure special exemption. Alfonso X the Wise of Castile in his *Siete Partidas* (1263) imposed a fine or lashing as the penalty for a Jew who neglected the order. In 1268 James I of Aragon exempted the Jews from wearing the badge, requiring them on the other hand to wear a round cape *(capa rotunda)*. In Castile, Henry III (1390–1406) yielded in 1405 to the demand of the Cortes

A typical hat worn by Jews in Spain. A panel from a page of *Las Cantigas de Santa Maria,* composed by Alfonso X of Castile (1252–1284). Madrid, Escorial Library, ms. T-I-1, Cant. 34.

and required even his Jewish courtiers to wear the badge. As a result of Vicente Ferrer's [41] agitation, the Jews were ordered in 1412 to wear distinctive clothing and a red badge, and they were further required to let their hair and beards grow long. The successors of Henry III renewed the decrees concerning the badge. In Aragon, John I, in 1393, prescribed special clothing for the Jews. In 1397, Queen Maria (the consort of King Martin) ordered all the Jews in Barcelona, both residents and visitors, to wear on their chests a circular patch of yellow cloth, a span in diameter,

[41] Dominican friar (c. 1350–1419)

with a red "bull's eye" in the center. They were to dress only in clothing of pale green color—as a sign of mourning for the ruin of their Temple, which they suffered because they had turned their backs upon Jesus—and their hats were to be high and wide with a short, wide *cuculla*. Violators were to be fined ten *libras* and stripped of their clothes wherever caught. When in 1400 King Martin granted the Jews of Lérida a charter of privileges, he required them, nevertheless, to wear the customary badge. In 1474, the burghers of Cervera sought to impose upon the local Jews a round badge of other than the customary form. In the period before the expulsion of the Jews from Spain in 1492, the wearing of the Jewish badge was almost universally enforced, and some persons demanded that it should be extended also to Conversos.

ITALY. Presumably the order of the Lateran Council was reenacted in Rome very soon after its promulgation in 1215, but it was certainly not consistently enforced. In 1221–22 the "enlightened" emperor Frederick II Hohenstaufen ordered all the Jews of the Kingdom of Sicily to wear a distinguishing badge of bluish color in the shape of the Greek letter τ and also to grow beards in order to be more easily distinguishable from non-Jews. In the same year the badge was imposed in Pisa and probably elsewhere. In the Papal States the obligation was first specifically imposed so far as is known by Alexander IV in 1257: there is extant a moving penitential poem written on this occasion by Benjamin b. Abraham Anav expressing the passionate indignation of the Roman Jews on this occasion. The badge here took the form of a circular yellow patch a handspan in diameter to be worn on a prominent place on the outer garment: for the women, two blue stripes on the veil. In 1360 an ordinance of the city of Rome required all male Jews, with the exception of physicians, to wear a coarse red cape, and all women to wear a red apron, and inspectors were appointed to enforce the regulation. Noncompliance was punished by a fine of 11 scudi; informers who pointed out offenders were entitled to half the fine. The ordinance

Circular badge worn by an Italian Jewish bridegroom. Bottom half of an initial word panel from the *Hamburg Halakhah Miscellany,* Padua, 1477. Hamburg, Staats- und Universitätsbibliothek, Cod. Heb. 337 (scrin 132) fol. 75v.

was revised in 1402, eliminating the reward for informing, and exempting the Jews from wearing the special garb inside the ghetto. In Sicily, there was from an early period a *custos rotulae* whose function it was to ensure that the obligation was not neglected. Elsewhere in Italy, however, the enforcement was sporadic, although it was constantly being demanded by fanatical preachers and sometimes temporarily enacted. The turning point came with the bull *Cum nimis absurdum* of Pope Paul IV in 1555, which inaugurated the ghetto system. This enforced the wearing of the badge (called by the Italian Jews *scimanno,* from Heb. *siman*) for the Papal States, later to be imitated throughout Italy (except in Leghorn), and enforced until the period of the French Revolution. In Rome, as well as in the Papal

The circular badge worn by Italian Jews. Detail from a 15th-century painting by an unknown Italian artist of the Madonna and Child. The four Jewish figures are Daniel Norsa and his family. Mantua, Church of Sant' Andrea. Photo Alinari, Florence.

States in the south of France, it took the form of a yellow hat for men, a yellow kerchief for women. In the Venetian dominions the color was red. In Candia (Crete), then under Venetian rule, Jewish shops had to be distinguished by the badge. David d'Ascoli, who published in 1559 a Latin protest against the degrading regulation, was severely punished and his work was destroyed.

GERMANY. In Germany and the other lands of the Holy Roman Empire, the pointed hat was first in use as a distinctive sign. It was not officially imposed until the second half of the 13th century (*Schwabenspiegel,* art. 214, c. 1275; *Weichbild-Vulgata,* art. 139, second half of 13th century; cf. Council of Breslau, 1267; Vienna, 1267; Olmuetz, 1342; Prague, 1355, etc.). The church councils of Breslau and Vienna, both held in 1267, required the Jews of Silesia, Poland, and Austria to wear not a badge but the pointed hat characteristic of Jewish garb (the *pileum cornutum*). A church council held in Ofen (Budapest) in 1279 decreed that the Jews were to wear on the chest a round patch in the form of a wheel. The badge was imposed for the first time in Augsburg in 1434, and its general enforcement was demanded by Nicolaus of Cusa[42] and John of Capistrano.[43] In 1530, the ordinance was applied to the

[42] German theologian and philosopher (1401–1464)
[43] Franciscan friar (1386–1456)

91

The German Jewish pointed hat as depicted in the *Regensburg Pentateuch,* a Hebrew illuminated manuscript, Germany, 1300. Jerusalem, Israel Museum, ms. 180/52, fol. 154v.

whole of Germany (*Reichspolizeiordnung,* art. 22). In the course of the 15th century, a Jewish badge, in addition to the Jewish hat, was introduced in various forms into

Germany. A church council which met in Salzburg in 1418

A German Jew and Jewess from Worms, 16th century, in typical Jewish dress with circular badges on their garments. Worms, Stadtarchiv.

ordered Jewish women to attach bells to their dresses so that their approach might be heard from a distance. In Augsburg in 1434 the Jewish men were ordered to attach yellow circles to their clothes, in front, and the women were ordered to wear yellow pointed veils. Jews on a visit to Nuremberg were required to wear a type of long, wide hood falling over the back, by which they would be distinguished from the local Jews. The obligation to wear the yellow badge was imposed upon all the Jews in Germany in 1530 and in Austria in 1551. As late as in the reign of Maria Theresa (1740–80) the Jews of Prague were required to wear yellow collars over their coats.

Discontinuance. In the new communities which became established in Western Europe (and later America) from the close of the 16th century under somewhat more free conditions the wearing of the Jewish badge was never imposed, though sometimes suggested by fanatics. In Poland, partly probably because the Jews constituted a distinct ethnic element, it was likewise virtually unknown except in some major cities under German influence. Similarly the Court Jews of Germany were unable to perform their function unless dressed like other people. In the course of the 18th century, although there was no official modification of the established policy, the wearing of the Jewish badge came to be neglected over a good part of Europe. In Venice the red hat continued to be worn by elderly persons and rabbis through sheer conservatism.

From the 17th century, there were some regional suspensions of the distinctive sign in Germany, as also for the Jews of Vienna in 1624, and for those of Mannheim in 1691. It was abrogated at the end of the 18th century with Jewish emancipation. Thus on Sept. 7, 1781, the yellow "wheel" was abolished by Emperor Joseph II in all the territories of the Austrian crown. In the Papal States in France the yellow hat was abolished in 1791 after the French Revolution reached the area, although some persons retained it until forbidden to do so by official proclamation. In the Papal States in Italy, on the other hand, the obligation was reimposed as late as 1793. When in 1796–97 the armies of the French Revolution entered Italy and the ghettos were abolished, the obligation to wear the Jewish badge disappeared. Its reimposition was threatened but not carried out during the reactionary period after the fall of Napoleon, and it then seemed that the Badge of Shame was only an evil memory of the past.

It was to commemorate the yellow badge or hat that Theodor Herzl chose this color for the cover of the first Zionist periodical *Die Welt.* It was in the same spirit that the *Juedische Rundschau,* the organ of the Zionist Organization in Germany, wrote on the morrow of the Nazi boycott of Jewish businesses on April 1, 1933: "Wear it with pride, this yellow badge" (no. 27, April 4, 1933).

Yellow Badge in the Nazi Period. In 1938 the Nazis compelled Jewish shopkeepers to display the words "Jewish business" in their windows but did not introduce distinctive signs to be worn by Jews until after the occupation of Poland. The first to issue an order on his own initiative, without awaiting instructions from the central authority, was the town Kommandant of Wloclawek, S.S. Oberfuehrer Cramer, who, on Oct. 24, 1939, ordered that every Jew in Wloclawek was to wear a distinctive sign on the back in the form of a yellow triangle at least 15 cm. in size. The order was published in the *Leslauer Bote* (Oct. 25, 1939). The order applied to all Jews, without distinction of age or sex. This device was rapidly adopted by other commanders in the occupied regions in the East and received official approval, in consideration of the anti-Semitic sentiments prevailing among the local Polish public, which received the new German measure with enthusiasm. The dates of application of the measure varied. There were regions where the instructions were applied even before they were issued in the General-Gouvernment, such as in Cracow, where the Jews were compelled to wear the sign from Nov. 18, 1939, whereas the date throughout the General-Gouvernment was Dec. 1, 1939. In Lvov, the order was applied as from July 15, 1941, and in eastern Galicia from Sept. 15, 1941. On the other hand, in certain places the instruction is known to have been applied only after publication of the general order, as for example in Warsaw on Dec. 12, 1939, and not on Dec. 1, 1939, even though Warsaw was included in the General-Gouvernment. In the smaller communities, the official German instructions were replaced by an announcement of the Judenrat.

In the West, the situation was totally different. In the *Reichsgebiet* (the territory of the Reich proper, as opposed to the occupied territories), the order was issued on Sept. 1, 1941. It was published in the *Reichsgesetzblatt* and was applied as from Sept. 19, 1941. This date was also valid for the Jews of Bohemia, Moravia, and Slovakia. The age from which the wearing of the sign was compulsory was six years 95

A Dutch Jewish woman wearing the yellow badge, 1942.
Jerusalem, Yad Vashem Archives.

for Germany and Western Europe and ten years for Eastern
Europe. In certain places the age differed. In Holland, the
order was applied as from May 1942, while in Belgium and
France the Jews were compelled to wear the distinctive sign

from June 1942. A meeting had been held in Paris in March 1942 to coordinate the application of the order in these three countries. In Bulgaria, the order was applied from September 1942, in Greece from February 1943, and in Hungary from April 1944. The type of distinctive sign varied, the following being the principal forms: a yellow Shield (Star) of David inscribed with *J* or *Jude,* etc.; a white armband with a blue Shield of David on it; a Shield of David, with or without inscription and in various colors; a yellow armband with or without inscription; a yellow button in the form of a Shield of David; a metal tag inscribed with the letter *J;* a yellow triangle; a yellow circle. This general use of the Shield of David as the Jewish badge was unknown in the Middle Ages. The inscriptions appearing on the badges were specially chosen to resemble Hebrew characters. After the Jews were compelled to reside in ghettos, they were also forced to wear the distinctive sign in conformity with the order applying to the region in which the ghetto was located. In the concentration camps they wore the sign which designated political prisoners on which was sewn a triangle or a yellow stripe to distinguish them from non-Jewish prisoners. In the *Reichsgebiet,* as well as in several of the occupied countries, the Germans introduced distinctive signs on Jewish business premises, passports, and ration cards, where the letter *J* was overprinted in a most conspicuous manner.

REACTIONS. Jews reacted with dignity to the order and wore the sign as if it were a decoration. However, they did not realize the danger which lay in wearing a distinctive sign. Non-Jews, especially in Eastern Europe, generally accepted this anti-Jewish measure with enthusiasm and saw in it an opportunity to remove the Jews from commercial, economic, and public life. In the West, reactions varied. The Jews could often rely on the hatred of the Germans by the public, and this even brought active support to the Jews. The Dutch wore the badge out of solidarity with the Jewish citizens. Three-hundred thousand replicas of the badge were produced and distributed throughout Holland bearing

A replica of the Dutch Jewish badge printed and distributed by the Dutch underground in 1942. The text reads: "Jews and non-Jews stand united in their struggle." Amsterdam, Jewish Historical Museum.

the inscription: "Jews and non-Jews stand united in their struggle!" In Denmark the badge was never introduced as a result of the courageous resistance of King Christian X, who was said to have threatened to wear it himself.

CONSEQUENCES. The principal objective in introducing distinctive signs for the Jews was to erect a barrier between them and non-Jews and to restrict their movements. The

Germans achieved this objective to a large extent, despite

Jewish badges decreed by the Nazis during their occupation of
Europe in World War II. 1. Bulgaria, Poland (part), Lithuania,
Hungary, Greece (part) (yellow star). 2. Germany, Alsace,
Bohemia-Moravia (black on yellow). 3. France (black on
yellow). 4. Holland (black on yellow). 5. Greece (part),
Serbia, Belgrade, Sofia (yellow armband). 6. Belgium (black
on yellow). 7. Slovakia (blue star on yellow background).
8. Bulgaria (black on yellow). 9. Slovakia (yellow star).
10. Poland (part), East and Upper Silesia (blue star on white
armband). Jerusalem, Yad Vashem Archives.

the various reactions which rendered application of the order difficult. The Jews increasingly concentrated in closed districts even before the establishment of the ghettos by the Nazis for fear of being arrested and deported to concentration camps. A Jew had the choice of concealing the sign and thus becoming an offender liable to a deportation sentence to the concentration camps, or of wearing the sign and becoming an easy prey to his enemies. The distinctive signs were thus an effective means in the hands of the Germans to facilitate their plan to exterminate the Jews.

4 DESECRATION OF THE HOST

Desecration of the Host is the alleged profanation of the wafer consecrated in the Roman Catholic ceremony of the Eucharist, and believed in the Catholic doctrine of Transubstantiation to become thereby the actual body of Jesus. The doctrine was first officially recognized at the Fourth Lateran Council of 1215. After that period therefore it was widely held that in certain circumstances—for instance disbelief or desecration—the Host might show supernatural powers. At the same time, it was imagined in some Christian circles that the Jews, believing paradoxically (which they obviously could not if they remained Jews) that the consecrated wafer was in fact the very body of Jesus, desired to renew upon it and him the agonies of the Passion, by stabbing, tormenting, or burning it. Such was the intensity of their paradoxical hatred that they would not abandon their Jewish perfidy even if the sacred wafer manifested its indignation and its miraculous essence by shedding blood, emitting voices, or even taking to flight. There is no need to regard as a wholly spiteful invention the statement that the consecrated wafer shed drops of blood, the most common manner in which the outrage became known, for a scarlet fungoid organism (called for this reason the *Micrococcus prodigiosus*) may sometimes form on stale food kept in a dry place, having an appearance not unlike blood. The charge of desecrating the Host was leveled against Jews all over the Roman Catholic world, frequently bringing in its train persecution and massacre.

The first recorded case of alleged Desecration of the Host was at Belitz near Berlin in 1243, when a number of Jews and Jewesses were burned at the stake on this charge on the spot later known as the Judenberg. It is significant that no cases or few are recorded in Italy, partly owing to the protective policies of the popes, partly to the skeptical nature of the Italian people (the best-known Italian case, the "miracle of Bolsena" (1264) involved a doubting priest, not a Jew). On the other hand, the most remarkable artistic representation of the Desecration of the Host was in the famous altar predella painted by Paolo Uccello (1397–1475) for the Confraternity of the Sacred Sacrament at Urbino, showing in successive panels the Jewish loan banker purchasing the wafer from a needy woman, his attempt to burn it, the miraculous manifestation that followed, and the subsequent terrible punishment by the burning at the stake of the culprit—with his wife, and their children. The Jews were expelled from England (1290) before the libel became widely spread; but there it received its reflection in the Croxton Sacrament Play, written long after the Expulsion (c. 1461).

Well-known incidents on the Continent were those of Paris in 1290, commemorated in the Church of the Rue des Billettes and in a local confraternity which long flourished; in Brussels (Enghien) in 1370, long celebrated in a special festivity and still in important artistic relics in the Church of St. Gudule, which led to the extermination of Belgian Jewry; at Deggendorf in Bavaria in 1337–38 which sparked off a series of massacres affecting scores of places in the region, still celebrated locally as the Deggendorf Gnad; at Knoblauch near Berlin in 1510 which resulted in 38 barbarous executions and the expulsion of Jews from Brandenburg (it was subsequently discovered that a common thief was responsible); at Segovia in 1415, said to have brought about an earthquake which resulted in the confiscation of the synagogue, the execution of leading Jews, and is still the occasion of the great local feast of Corpus Christi. The Infante Don Juan of Aragon took under his personal patronage allegations of the sort at Barcelona in 1367 (when some of the greatest Jewish scholars of the age, including Ḥasdai Crescas and Isaac

102

assaw Von den Juden als hernach volgt
hye tragen die Jude vn schulklopffer.
die sacrament yn ir synagog. vnd vber
antwurten oye den Juden.

hye stycht pfeyl Jud das sacrament
auff irem altar.ist plut darauß gangen
das er vn ander iuden gesehen haben.

hye vecht man all Juden zu Passaw
die oy sacramét gekauffi verschickt ge
stolen vnd verprant haben.

hye furt in sy fur-gericht. verurtaylt
die vier getauffi. fackel mand. kolman
vnd walich.sein gekopft worden.

German broadsheet, c. 1480, telling the story of the alleged
desecration of the Host in Passau, Bavaria, in 1478.
3. The Jews take the Host to the synagogue. 4. In reenactment of the
crucifixion they stab the wafers, out of which blood flows.

B. Sheshet Perfet, were implicated) and in Teruel and
Huesca ten years later.

The   Marranos[44] of Spain and Portugal were also
popularly believed to continue the malpractice of their
Jewish predecessors in this respect. When in 1671 the pyx
with a consecrated host was stolen from the Church of
Orivellas in Lisbon (by a common thief as subsequently
transpired) the court went into mourning and an edict was
signed banishing all New Christians from the country.
Even in the 18th century, an Alsatian Jew was cruelly
executed with others on a charge of desecrating the Host
(Nancy 1761). The accusation was brought up in Rumania
(Bislad) as late as 1836.

[44] Descendants of Jews in Spain and Portugal whose ancestors had been
converted to Christianity under pressure but who secretly observed Jewish
rituals

5 WANDERING JEW

The Wandering Jew is a figure in Christian legend condemned to wander by Jesus until his second coming for having rebuffed or struck him on his way to the crucifixion. The story has given rise to many folktales and literature still flourishing into the 20th century. Like the image of the Jew in popular conception, the personality of and tales about the Wandering Jew reflect the beliefs and tastes of the age in which he is described. While in the era of Church dominion he inspires religious horror and exhortations to piety, the character is later used as a vehicle for social satire, and even appears as a tragic figure expressing a spirit of revolt against the Church and the established order. He also appears in his old role as a target for modern anti-Semitism. The name Wandering Jew has been given to a card game, a game of dice, plants, and birds. The legend has obvious affinities with other tales of eternal wanderers, primarily Cain (with whom the Jewish people as a whole are identified by Christian homilists beginning with Tertullian (150–230)).

Origin. At first the legend had only indirect connections with the Jews. Its beginnings have been traced (by L. Neubauer, see bibliography) to the New Testament story of the high priest's officer who struck Jesus (John 18:20–22); it subsequently became linked and equated with other figures and elements, and in particular was associated with sayings attributed to Jesus foretelling his second coming (Mat. 16:28; John 21:20). The legend changed, and details were added. This story of the sinner doomed to eternal life apparently circulated in oral tradition in the Near East and eastern Mediterranean as late as the 15th century.

When the legend appeared in Europe it readily gave expression to the prevailing medieval anti-Jewish hostility. The first written account specifically mentioning a Jew condemned for his sin to live until Jesus' second coming is recorded in a 13th-century chronicle of Bolognese origin. This states that in 1223 some pilgrims at the monastery of Ferrara related "that they had seen a certain Jew in Armenia who had been present at the Passion of the Lord, and, as He was going to His martyrdom, drove Him along wickedly with these words 'Go, go thou tempter and seducer, to receive what you have earned.' Jesus is said to have answered him: 'I go, and you will await me until I come again.'" The Jew subsequently repented of the deed, converted to Christianity, and led an ascetic life while enduring his punishment (*Ignoti Monachi Cisterciencis S. Mariae de Ferraria Chronica* . . . ed. A. Gandenzi, 1888). The English chronicler Roger of Wendover relates in his *Flores Historiarum* for 1228 that an Armenian bishop visiting the monastery of St. Albans told substantially the same story, adding that the man had struck Jesus. The tale was incorporated by Matthew Paris (d. 1259) in his widely circulated *Chronica Majora*, and in many other writings—in entirety or mentioned—in chronicles, poems, tractates, pilgrim itineraries, and miracle plays, from the 13th to 16th centuries in Italy, Spain, France, and England. The scene with Jesus is said to have been painted by Andrea Vanni of Siena (d. 1414).

At the beginning of the 17th century a chapbook was printed in German which accentuated the anti-Jewish implications of the legend, and was to popularize it further and inaugurate its transposition to further literary genres. Evidently based on Matthew Paris' chronicle, it first appeared under different imprints in Germany dated 1602, entitled *Kurtze Beschreibung und Erzehlung von einen Juden mit Namen Ahasverus*. In the copy published under the imprint of "Christoff Creutzer of Leyden" it is related that Paulus von Eitzen, bishop of Schleswig, in the winter of 1542, when attending church in Hamburg, saw a tall man, dressed in threadbare garments, with long hair, standing barefoot in the chancel; whenever the name of Jesus was pronounced he bowed his head, beat his breast, and sighed profoundly. It was reported that he was a shoemaker named Ahasuerus who had cursed Jesus on his way to the

French broadsheet with a poem on the Wandering Jew, here called Isaac Laquedem, Nancy, 1850s. Cecil Roth Collection.

The release of the Wandering Jew on Judgment Day, one of the series of wood engravings, "The Legend of the Wandering Jew," by Gustav Doré, 1856.

crucifixion. On further questioning he related the historical events that had occurred since. He conversed in the language of the country he happened to be visiting. This version shows "Ahasuerus" as a fully fledged personification of the Jewish people, incorporating the themes of participation in the crucifixion, condemnation to eternal suffering until Jesus' second coming, and the bearing of witness to the truth of the Christian tradition. The description of his person suggests the well-known figure of the Jewish peddler.

In former versions of the legend the man who assailed Jesus is referred to by various names: Cartaphilus, Buttadeus, Buttadeo, Boutedieu, Votadio, Juan Espera en Dios. Subsequently the name Ahasuerus (then a cant name for Jew through the familiarity it achieved in Purim plays) became the most common appellation of the Wandering Jew in later literature, though in French he is frequently called Isaac Laquedem (corrupted Hebrew for "Isaac the Old" or "from the East"). In the German connotation he appears in a distinctly anti-Jewish light, referred to as the "Eternal Jew" (Ger. *Der ewige Jude*), which in English and French versions became the "Wandering Jew" *(le Juif errant)*.

Numerous reissues of the chapbook appeared in German in varying versions in the 17th century, nine of which are attributed to the authorship of a (pseudonymous) Chrystostum Dudulaeus Westphalus. It was translated or paraphrased into French (notably the *Histoire admirable du juif errant*, c. 1650, reprinted well into the 19th century), Danish (*Sandru Beskriffuelse*, 1621), Swedish (*Jerusalems Skomager*, 1643), Estonian (printed at Reval, 1613), and Italian (*Narrazione d'un Giudeo errante*, and others).

In Folktale. Well over 100 folktales have invested the legend of the Wandering Jew with many local variations in places far apart, e.g., when the moon is old, he is very very old, but when the moon is young he turns young again (Ukraine); he may only rest for as long as it takes to eat a morsel of white bread (Westphalia), and can only rest on two harrows or a plowshare (Denmark, Sweden). Throughout the Alps his appearance presaged some calamity. In France his passing was connected with storm, epidemics, or famine; 19th-century museums in Ulm and Berne even exhibited large shoes allegedly worn by the Wandering Jew. Mark Twain in his *Innocents Abroad* (1869) summarizes a local version of the legend told in Jerusalem by his guide in the Via Dolorosa.

After 1600 the Jew was reported to have made his appearance in localities in numerous countries at various dates (among many: Luebeck, 1603; Paris, 1604; Brussels, 1640; Leipzig, 1642; Munich, 1721; London, 1818).

6 THE GHETTO

Establishment of the Ghetto. From the beginning of the 16th century the name given in Italy to the Jewish quarter, which was separated and closed off by law from the other parts of the town by a wall and gates, was "ghetto." From then on, the word ghetto has also been used to designate Jewish quarters which were officially set aside in other countries. Figuratively and erroneously, this name has also been regularly applied to quarters, neighborhoods, and areas throughout the Diaspora, which became places of residence for numerous Jews.

The root of the word ghetto has been sought in Hebrew (*get*—"bill of divorcement"), in Yiddish, Latin, Greek, and Gothic. There is, however, no doubt that the origin is *geto nuovo* ("the new foundry"), the site of the first separate Jewish quarter in Venice from 1516. The Jews of Italy occasionally referred to the ghetto in their dialect as *get* but the usual appellation was "courtyard." In the towns of southern France under papal rule where ghettos were established after the Italian model, they were named *carrière* in French and *mesillah* ("road") in Hebrew.

The idea of the ghetto in its restricted sense resulted from the tendency implanted in Christianity from the fourth to fifth centuries to isolate the Jews and humiliate them. It first appears in the West in the proceedings of the Church Councils of the Middle Ages, especially at the third Lateran council (1179), where Jews and Christians were prohibited from living together. Initially, this prohibition was enforced in a few places, as in London from 1276. From the beginning of the 15th century it was included—in conjunction with the prohibition on moneylending against interest

The ghetto of Venice, 1960s. Photo Joseph Shaw, London.

and the order concerning the Jewish badge –in the anti-Jewish program of the Christian religious orders, especially in Italy; it was thus applied, for example, in Bologna from 1417 and in Turin from 1425. However, the ghetto did not appear as a permanent institution until its introduction in Venice in 1516. Then Jews who sought refuge in the city, from which they had been banned over a lengthy period, were admitted on condition that they live in the *geto nuovo* quarter, an isolated island among the canals of Venice which could easily be completely cut off from its surroundings by a wall, gates, and drawbridges. In 1541, the *geto vecchio* ("the old foundry") quarter was added for the integration of Jews from oriental countries, and the whole area was from then on known as the "ghetto."

In 1555, Pope Paul IV in his bull *Cum nimis absurdum* ordered that the anti-Jewish program of the monks of establishing ghettos should be applied in Rome and the Papal States. On July 26, 1555, which fell on the Ninth of Av, Jews of Rome were compelled to move to the new quarter on the left bank of the Tiber River; the area was immediately surrounded by a wall to isolate it from the city. After a short while, this innovation was also introduced in 111

Painting of the Rome Ghetto by E. Roesler Franz (1845–1907).
Rome, Museo di Roma.

the other towns of the Papal States, and from 1562 the new
institution became known, even officially, by the name of
the Jewish quarter of Venice—"ghetto."

Pressure was also exerted on the other rulers of the
Italian states to introduce the ghetto (in Tuscany in
1570–71; in Padua in 1601–03; in Verona in 1599; in the
duchy of Mantua in 1612; etc.) so that the ghetto institution
was finally established throughout Italy, with the exception
of Leghorn.

The ghetto introduced by Christians was accompanied
by imposition of the badge, compulsory attendance of Jews
at conversionary sermons, restriction of the professions
they were authorized to practice, and other humiliations.
Generally, the authorities did not allow extension of the
ghetto boundaries, even when the population had increased; the ghettos were therefore crowded and unsanitary.
For the same reason, additional stories were continually
built onto the existing houses and the buildings were in
constant danger of collapse; misfortunes occasionally

occurred, and when fires broke out, severe damage was caused to the ghettos.

According to papal decree, when a ghetto was established it was to have one gate only. In fact, however, it usually had two or three gates. These were guarded by Christian gatekeepers, whose salaries the Jews were compelled to pay; they were closed at night and on all important Christian festivals, including the Easter period, from the Thursday until the Sunday of Holy Week. At night and during Christian festivals, no Jew was permitted to leave the ghetto. In several smaller localities, all the houses in the ghetto were connected to each other by passages and doors to facilitate movement in times of emergency. Non-Jewish landlords were not permitted to raise the rents, and the rights of Jewish tenants were protected by *ḥazakah* ("established claim"), an ancient institution recognized by Italian law (under the name *jus gazaga*). Although Jews were not allowed to acquire the houses in which they lived, the right of *ḥazakah* could be sold, purchased, or bequeathed, as though it was an actual property right. The ghetto, as all Jewish quarters in all periods, was an almost autonomous town and the institutions of the Jewish community operated within its boundaries; at times, the communal life of the ghetto was better organized than that of the Christian town in which it was situated. There were even Jews who did not ignore the positive aspects of the ghetto. In Verona and Mantua it was customary to commemorate the anniversary of its establishment by a special prayer in the synagogue.

Toward the close of the 18th century, the severity of the ghetto regime was somewhat alleviated in several of the Italian states. In 1796 the armies of the French Republic tore down the ghetto walls of all the Italian towns. However, the ghettos were reestablished after the fall of Napoleon in 1815 but not with the same measure of stringency. The ghetto walls were only rebuilt in Rome, Modena, and a few other towns. With the consolidation of the liberal regime in Italy during the 19th century, the 113 ghetto was again abolished, although there were still some occasional periods of reaction here and there. The gates of the Rome ghetto were destroyed in 1848; the right of residence of the Jews was, however, officially restricted to a special quarter until the fall of the papal regime in 1870. Outside Italy, the ghetto—in the original sense of the Italian term—was only enforced in the provinces under papal rule in southern France, in several German towns, and in a few places in East Europe. In detail, there were always considerable differences between them.

The old Jewish quarter of Boskovice, Moravia, to which Jews were first restricted in 1727. Courtesy Czechoslovak State Archives, Prague.

In Muslim Countries. Well before the advent of Islam the preference of religious and ethnic groups to live together in their own streets was commonly known in the Orient. These streets finally became distinct quarters. The quarters in which the majority of the population was Jewish were usually given the name of *ḥārat al-yahūd,* which literally translated from the Arabic means "Jewish Quarter," or simply *shara* and *al-ḥāra* as in Tunisia, Algeria, and Tripolitania. In Persia they were known as *maḥallat al-Yahūd,* in the Balkans as *maḥalla,* while in Yemen they were named *qāʿat al-Yahūd;* the term *mashata* (namely, the place where those who observe the Sabbath live) was also employed. The Jews themselves sometimes called their quarters *shekhunat ha-Yehudim,* the Hebrew equivalent of the various above-mentioned names. Barring a few exceptions, the Jewish quarters of Muslim countries had nothing in common with the ghettos of Christian countries. These quarters were not surrounded by a wall and did not have a gate which was closed at night, on the Sabbath, or on the Festivals. When such a wall existed, it was often because the whole town was divided into several separate quarters which were partitioned off from each other by a wall which contained one or two gates; the gates were closed from dusk to dawn for security reasons or upon the order of the police. In the Ottoman Empire the Jews were not compelled to live separately from the other inhabitants. The sole exception to this practice was in Yemen. Even when there were Jewish quarters, Jewish families lived alone or in groups in the other quarters, dispersed among the Muslims. As early as the Middle Ages many Jews of Baghdad lived in houses situated beyond the two quarters of the town where most of them had their dwellings. During the 12th century most of the Jews of Fez lived in the north of the city, in a quarter which had been given to them when the town was founded at the beginning of the ninth century. There were, however, many others who lived in the center of the town, well inside the Muslim quarter. Those whose houses were directly adjacent to the Great Mosque were dispossessed when it was decided to enlarge the structure. They were indemnified for their losses and they left the site. During the era of its splendor, Kairouan had a Jewish quarter, but it appears to have been a common occurrence for Jews to live outside this quarter. In Muslim Spain the Jews often lived among the other inhabitants. The fortified Jewish quarters did not 115 become the general rule until the country was reconquered by the Christian Spaniards. During that period, however, there were also Muslims who lived in quarters with a Jewish majority. Muslims were never forbidden to live in the Jewish quarters. Any difficulties, rather, arose from rabbinic laws which disapproved of the sale or rental of dwellings in the Jewish street to a gentile and granted priority rights over these dwellings to any Jew from the neighborhood. On the other hand, private houses belonging to Jews and Christians were to be found in all the quarters of the town. For this reason the Muslim religious authorities would not allow these houses to be higher than the neighboring mosque or the houses of the "believers."

In Muslim countries, the Covenant of Omar did not stipulate the physical separation of the Jews from the "faithful" (the Muslims), neither in towns nor in villages. On the contrary, in order to propagate their religion, the early Muslim theologians recommended that the "unbelievers" (Jews and Christians) be encouraged to live in all the quarters of the large towns. They said that they would thus become acquainted with the religion of the Prophet Muhammad by observing the lives of its believers at every moment. There were only a few Muslim jurists of the later periods who advised that non-Muslims be confined to separate quarters. Until the beginning of the 15th century, however, the orthodox Muslim rulers or their representatives had never officially prescribed the establishment of special quarters for the members of other religions. It was only in Egypt, and then only for a short while at the beginning of the 11th century, that the Fatimid caliph al-Ḥākim, who had suddenly become insane, confined all the Jews of Cairo to the Bāb-Zuwayla quarter. In the eastern part of the Muslim world, in the countries dominated by the Shiʿites (non-orthodox Muslims), the Jews were compelled to live in special quarters which resembled the European ghettos. In Persia, as in Afghanistan and the surrounding regions, the Jewish quarter was not only isolated behind a high wall but its inhabitants were also not authorized to own any shops beyond it. The Jews of Persia remained in their ghettos until recently, even though there was no law which forced them to do so.

In Morocco the term mellah, which designates the Jewish quarter, was originally the name of the site to the south of Fez-Jaïd on which the first special quarter for Jews in Morocco was actually established (probably in 1438). This mellah was and has since remained a special quarter surrounded by a wall and distinctly separated from the surrounding quarters. The segregation of all the Jews of Fez into its area was ordered. It was thus a ghetto, the first and, for a long time, the only one in Morocco. It was not until 1557 that a second ghetto was established in the country, in Marrakesh. Approximately 125 years later a third mellah was created in Meknès, and in 1808 four new ghettos were simultaneously erected in the principal ports of Morocco, in Tetuán, Salé, Rabat, and Mogador. The sharif granted the Jews of these towns one year in which they could sell their houses in the different quarters and build new ones in the mellah. The only exception made was for some 20 eminent families of Mogador, who continued to occupy their luxurious houses in the same residential quarter as that of the Muslim and Christian notables. In 1808 the Jews of Tetuán were compelled to move into a mellah because the sultan wished to erect a mosque in a street which was inhabited by them. At the same time, the sultan exploited the proximity of the Jewish houses to the mosque of Salé as a pretext to order the Jews of this town to live in a special quarter. The Jews of Morocco considered the creation of each mellah as a catastrophe; they therefore hastily abandoned it as soon as they had the means or the possibility. From the beginning of the 20th century, only the poor Jews continued to live in the mellahs. The name mellah was at first given, after Fez, to the few ghettos mentioned above and then to a few other quarters in other towns which were inhabited by the Jewish masses. The mellah of Casablanca, for example, did not have the characteristics of a ghetto. The decline of Muslim power

Scene in the mellah of Agoin, Morocco, 1953. Jerusalem,
Israel Museum Photo Collection. Department of Ethnography.
Photo Shulman.

generally resulted in the impoverishment of the Jewish
communities, whose quarters reflected this situation. These
quarters were often overpopulated. These ghettos, however,
always contained a few well-kept streets with very large and
beautiful houses, the properties of wealthy citizens, as was
the case in Fez and Marrakesh.

In 1728 and 1731 the Ottoman authorities ordered the
Jews of Istanbul (Constantinople) to leave the quarters
where they lived, under the pretext that their presence in
these quarters profaned the sanctity of the neighboring
118 mosques; but the Jews were not enclosed in a ghetto,

they merely went to live in other quarters. In 1679 the Jews of Yemen were expelled from the towns in which they had lived until then, and they were only authorized to establish themselves outside these cities, in special quarters. In the Islamic countries the two holy cities Mecca and Medina, as also the whole of the Hejaz, are prohibited to non-Muslims. Between the 13th and 15th centuries, for example, such Maghreb towns as Bougie, Gafsa, and Tebessa were, with intermissions, forbidden to non-Muslims. From the ninth century until the present the town of Moulay Idris, in Morocco, could not be visited by the "unbelievers." Kairouan, once a great Jewish center, remained out of bounds to non-Muslims from the 13th century until the end of the 19th century. On the other hand, some towns were exclusively, or in their majority, inhabited by Jews. This was the case with Lucena in Muslim Spain, Aghmat-Ailan (near Marrakesh) in Morocco, and Tamentit in the Algerian Sahara until 1492. Many other examples exist.

7 EXPULSIONS

The Jews underwent expulsions during the time of the Assyrian and Babylonian kingdoms. Pagan Rome also adopted on rare occasions a policy of removing the Jews from the capital, considering them an undesirable element: there is some vague information on the expulsion of the Jews from Rome in 139 B.C.E. among the other "Chaldeans." In 19 C.E. Tiberius ordered the expulsion of all the Jews in Italy if they would not abandon their faith. In 50 C.E. Claudius expelled them from Rome. From the end of the Bar Kokhba Revolt (135 C.E.) until the capture of Jerusalem by the Muslims (638), the Jews were prohibited from entering that city and its boundaries. The policy of expelling Jews was however only adopted by victorious Christianity from the fourth century C.E., in implementation of its objectives to separate the Jews from the rest of society, and degrade and oppress them so that they would convert to Christianity. Individual expulsions from Islamic countries, such as the expulsion from Tlemcen (N. Africa), are also recorded during the tenth century.

The phenomenon of expulsions is overwhelmingly found in Christian lands. Some of these were "general expulsions" which removed the Jews from the territory of a whole country for an extended period. The expulsion from England in 1290 (the number of expelled has been estimated at 16,000) removed the Jews from its borders until after 1650. The expulsions from France, especially those of 1306 and 1394, evicted the Jews from most of the territory within the borders of France until 1789. The expulsions from Spain and Portugal, 1492–97 (where the number of victims has been assessed by historians from

100,000 to several hundreds of thousands), removed the Jews from the Iberian peninsula almost until the present day and brought about a series of expulsions of Jews from lands within the sphere of influence of these countries. At the time of the Black Death (1348–50), the Jews were expelled from many places in Europe, but in most localities, especially in Germany, they were readmitted after a short while. The presence of Jews was rigorously prohibited in Russia from the 15th century until 1772, when masses of Jews accrued to Russia from the annexed Polish-Lithuanian territories. Even after this date, there was an attempt to maintain this prohibition in the form of the Pale of Settlement until 1917. Within the framework of its enforcement numerous expulsions of both groups of Jews and entire communities from towns and villages which were "out of bounds" (such as the expulsion from Moscow in 1891) were carried out. There were also expulsions of short duration from the boundaries of entire countries, such as the expulsion from Lithuania in 1495. Expulsions from specific regions and towns were frequent and regular occurrences in Germany and northern Italy during the 14th to 16th centuries, but in certain cases they were also revoked (for example the expulsion from Bohemia and Moravia, 1744–5). The political fragmentation of these countries during the Middle Ages usually enabled the Jews to settle within the proximity of the baronage or town from which they had been expelled and to return there after a short interval. During World War I, the Russian authorities evacuated about 600,000 Jews from Poland, Lithuania, and the Baltic countries to the interior of Russia, an act regarded as an expulsion.

While the motives for the expulsions fall into differing and variegated categories, the root of them all was hatred of the Jew. This hatred was at times exploited by fiscal considerations of the rulers responsible for the expulsions. Socio-economic factors contributed to the hostility of the Christian merchants and craftsmen toward their Jewish rivals, the hatred of Christian debtors for the Jewish 121

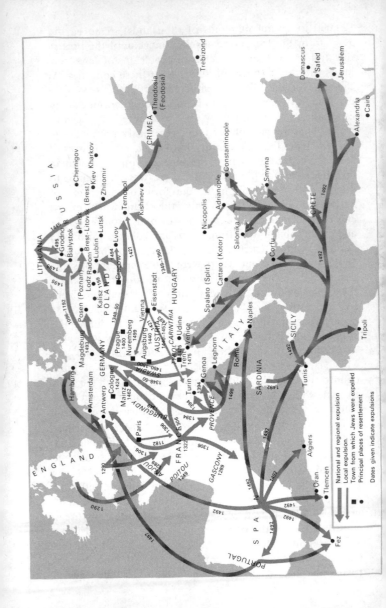

Trebizond

Theodosia (Feodosia)

CRIMEA

Damascus • Safed
Jerusalem

Chernigov
Pinsk (Brest) • Kiev Kharkov
Zhitomir

Alexandria • Cairo

RUSSIA

LITHUANIA

Grodno Lutsk
Bialystok Lublin
Posen (Poznan) Lodz Radom Brest-Litovsk Lvov Kishinev
Kalisz 1189 Krakow

Constantinople
Adrianople Smyrna

Ternopol

1495

POLAND

1421

Nicopolis Salonika

CRETE

1492

1349-1360

HUNGARY

Corfu

1492

Magdeburg Eisenstadt
1493 Prague Vienna
Nuremberg 1440 1421 CARINTHIA Cattaro (Kotor)
GERMANY 1499 Augsburg 1450-1452 Spalato (Split)
Hamburg Mainz 1400 AUSTRIA Udine
Amsterdam 1462 1348-50 SWABIA Trent Venice 1475
Antwerp Cologne 1424 1348-50 Turin 1485
1182 1394 Genoa Leghorn Naples
Paris 1306 1346 PROVENCE 1394 Rome ITALY
FRANCE 1306 1322 1498 SICILY
1290 1306 Tripoli
ENGLAND ANJOU 1289
POITOU
1290 GASCONY SARDINIA 1492
1249 1289 Tunis
1492
Algiers 1492
Oran 1492
SPAIN Tlemcen 1492

1492

PORTUGAL

Fez

Legend:

National and regional expulsion
Local expulsion
■ Town from which Jews were expelled
● Principal places of resettlement
Dates given indicate expulsions

moneylenders, and, on the other hand, the occasional feeling that there was no need for the Jews as moneylenders for interest and that they did not fulfill any other economic-social function. Tendencies and sentiments of national and political consolidation also played their part. In Spain, the desire to isolate the New Christians from Jewish influence was also a factor in the expulsion. In an epoch when the menace of death hovered continually over the Jews, especially in places where they had grown accustomed to expulsion and rapid readmission, expulsion was considered the lightest of possible evils. Judah Loew b. Bezalel (the Maharal of Prague) thought that the era of exile in which he lived was more tolerable because its principal sufferings consisted of expulsions, which he described as the divorce of a woman by her husband. The Jews of Frankfort, when they were actually expelled, also felt that "we went in joy and in sorrow; because of the destruction and the disgrace, we grieved for our community and we rejoiced that we had escaped with so many survivors" (poem by R. Elhanan b. Abraham Helin, at end of pt. 3 of *Zemah David*, 1692). The general expulsions were however considered disasters, and the expulsion from Spain in particular became a fearful memory for the nation. The expulsions always resulted in losses to property and damage to body and spirit. In addition to the losses caused by forced sales—when the buyer realized that the Jew was compelled to abandon all his real property, and at times many of his movable goods—insecurity and vagrancy left their imprint on the social and economic life of the Jews, especially in the German and Italian states. Highway robberies and losses suffered during the enforced travels also increased the damage to property. Much information is available on attacks and murders committed against expelled Jews who left their country and the protection of the authorities. Even in those expulsions where instructions were given to protect the departing Jews, such as the expulsions from England and Spain, there were numerous attacks. The wanderings were the cause of many diseases 123 and also reduced the natural increase. A shocking description of the sufferings of the exiles from Spain and Portugal is given in the writings of the kabbalist Judah b. Jacob Ḥayyat. He relates of himself and his companions after they had reached the safety of Muslim Tunis: "We ate the grass of the fields, and every day I ground with my own hands in the house of the Ishmaelites for the thinnest slice of bread not even fit for a dog. During the nights, my stomach was close to the ground—and my belly my cushion. Because of the great cold of the autumn—we had no garments in the frost and no houses to lodge in—we dug trenches in the refuse heaps of the town and put our bodies therein" (introduction to *Minḥat Yehudah* (Mantua, 1558), 3a).

The expulsions left their impress on the entire nation and its history, both materially and spiritually. They maintained and constantly intensified the feeling of foreignness of the Jews in the Diaspora. The consecutive expulsions from England, France, and Spain resulted in a situation where after 1492 there were no Jews living openly on the European coast of the Atlantic Ocean in a period when this had become the center of world traffic. The expulsions of the late 15th century resulted in the return of many Jews to the Islamic countries, in particular to the Ottoman Empire. The Jews were also driven into Poland-Lithuania. Frequently, the expulsions caused the centers of gravity of Jewish life to be removed from one place to another, the creation of new centers of settlement, messianic movements, and a renewed relationship with Ereẓ Israel; it was no coincidence that the kabbalists of Safed were Spanish exiles. The expulsions also caused the Jews of Spain to come into contact with those of Italy, the Balkans, Asia Minor, North Africa, and many Middle Eastern countries, where they influenced and fashioned the social-spiritual character of many communities in these regions. The expulsions may be considered one of the decisive factors shaping the map of Jewish settlement and one of the forces which molded the thinking of Jews both in relation to themselves and to the world of nations and states which surrounded them.

8 POGROMS

The word pogrom is of Russian origin designating an attack, accompanied by destruction, the looting of property, murder, and rape, perpetrated by one section of the population against another. In modern Russian history pogroms have been perpetrated against other nations (Armenians, Tatars) or groups of inhabitants (intelligentsia). However, as an international term, the word "pogrom" is employed in many languages to describe specifically the attacks accompanied by looting and bloodshed against the Jews in Russia. The word designates more particularly the attacks carried out by the Christian population against the Jews between 1881 and 1921 while the civil and military authorities remained neutral and occasionally provided their secret or open support. The pogroms occurred during periods of severe political crises in the country and were outbreaks linked to social upheavals and nationalist incitement in Eastern Europe. (Similar events also occurred during that period, though on a more limited scale, in the context of the anti-Semitic movements in Germany, Austria, Rumania, and the Balkan countries, and of nationalist and religious fanaticism in Morocco, Algeria, and Persia.)

The Jews of Russia were the victims of three large-scale waves of pogroms, each of which surpassed the preceding in scope and savagery. These occurred between the years 1881 and 1884, 1903 and 1906, and 1917 and 1921. There were outbreaks in Poland after it regained independence in 1918, and in Rumania from 1921.

In the 1880s. The pogroms of the 1880s took place during the period of confusion which prevailed in Russia after the 125 assassination of Czar Alexander II by members of the revolutionary organization Narodnaya Volya on March 13, 1881. Anti-Jewish circles spread a rumor that the czar had been assassinated by Jews and that the government authorized attacks on them. The pogroms at first also received the support of some revolutionary circles, who regarded this action as a preliminary awakening of the masses which would lead to the elimination of the existing regime. The first pogrom occurred in the town of Yelizavetgrad (Kirovograd), in Ukraine, at the end of April 1881. From there, the pogrom wave spread to the surrounding villages and townlets—about 30 in number. At the beginning of May, the pogroms spread to the provinces of Kherson, Taurida, Yekaterinoslav (Dnepropetrovsk), Kiev, Poltava, and Chernigov. The most severe attack was perpetrated in Kiev over three days before the eyes of the governor-general and his staff of officials and police force while no attempt was made to restrain the rioters. The pogroms in Odessa were of more limited scope. During the months of July and August there was again a series of pogroms in the provinces of Chernigov and Poltava. During this period, the pogroms were mainly restricted to destruction, the looting of property, and beatings. The number of dead was small. The attackers came from among the rabble of the towns, the peasants, and the workers in industrial enterprises and the railroads. At the end of this period, the government forces reacted against the rioters and in several places even opened fire on them, leaving a number of dead and injured. The pogroms occurred in a restricted geographical region—southern and eastern Ukraine. Here there was a combination of aggravating circumstances: the traditional rebelliousness among the masses, a tradition of anti-Jewish hatred and persecutions from the 17th and 18th centuries (the massacres perpetrated by Chmielnicki and the Haidamacks), together with the presence there of homeless seasonal workers in the factories, railways, and ports, the rise of a rural bourgeoisie and local intelligentsia, who regarded the Jews as most dangerous rivals, and an extremist revolutionary movement which was unscrupulous in the methods it adopted.

After the pogroms in the spring and summer of 1881, there was a remission, although occasional pogroms broke out in various parts of the country. Among these was a severe pogrom in Warsaw on the Catholic Christmas Day and an Easter pogrom in Balta, in which two Jews were killed, 120 injured, and many cases of rape occurred. In Belorussia and Lithuania, where the local authorities adopted a firm attitude against the rioters, large fires broke out in many towns and townlets; a considerable number of these were started by the enemies of the Jews. The murder of individual Jews and even whole families also became a common occurrence during this period. On June 21, 1882, the new minister of the interior, Count D. Tolstoy, published an order which placed the blame for the pogroms on the governors of the provinces and declared that "every attitude of negligence on the part of the administration and the police would entail the dismissal from their position of those who were guilty." Isolated pogroms nevertheless occurred during the following two years or so. In the spring of 1883, a sudden wave of pogroms broke out in the towns of Rostov and Yekaterinoslav and their surroundings. On this occasion, the authorities reacted with vigor against the rioters and there were several victims among them. The last great outburst occurred in June 1884 in Nizhni Novgorod (now Gorki), where the mob attacked the Jews of the Kanavino quarter, killing nine of them and looting much property. The authorities tried over 70 of the rioters and severe penalties of imprisonment were imposed on them. This marked the end of the first wave of pogroms in Russia.

The pogroms of the 1880s greatly influenced the history of Russian Jewry. In their wake, the Russian government adopted a systematic policy of discrimination with the object of removing the Jews from their economic and public positions. This was achieved either by restrictive laws (the May Laws of 1882, the percentage norm of admission (numerus clausus) to secondary schools, higher institu- 127 tions of learning, etc.) or by administrative pressure, which reached its climax with the expulsion of the Jews from Moscow in 1891–92. A mass Jewish emigration began from Russia to the United States and other countries. One reaction to the pogroms was the birth of a nationalist and a Zionist movement among the Russian Jews, while many of the Jewish youth joined the revolutionary movement. The year 1881, the first year of the pogroms, was a turning point not only for Russian Jewry but also for the whole of the Jewish people.

1903 to 1906. The second wave of pogroms was connected with the revolutionary agitation in Russia and the first Russian revolution of 1905. In its struggle against the revolutionary movement, the Russian government gave the reactionary press a free hand to engage in unbridled anti-Jewish incitement in an attempt to divert the anger of the masses against the Jews and to represent the revolutionary movement as the result of "Jewish machinations." Monarchist societies, such as the Union of Russian People, the Double-headed Eagle Society, and others, which were referred to by the general name of the Black Hundreds, played a prominent role in the organization of the pogroms. The first results of this incitement were pogroms which occurred in Kishinev during Passover 1903, in the wake of the wild agitation propagated by the anti-Semitic local newspaper *Bessarabets,* edited by P. Krushevan. This pogrom was accompanied by savage murder (over 50 dead, hundreds injured) and mutilation of the injured and dead. About 1,500 Jewish houses and shops were looted. The pogrom angered public opinion throughout the world. Subsequently, a self-defense movement was organized among the Jewish youth. Its organizers were mainly drawn from the Zionist socialist parties and the Bund. In a pogrom which broke out in Gomel in September 1903, the self-defense group played a prominent part in saving Jewish lives and property. In the fall of 1904, a series of pogroms was perpetrated in Smela, Rovno, Aleksandriya and other places by army recruits about to be sent to the war against Japan and by the local rabble. In 1905, when the revolutionary movement gained strength, reactionary circles, with the support of the government, intensified the anti-Jewish propaganda, and an atmosphere of terror reigned in many towns of the Pale of Settlement and beyond it. Occasionally pogroms occurred in reaction to revolutionary demonstrations, which the opponents of the revolution condemned as Jewish demonstrations. In February 1905 a pogrom took place in Feodosiya, and in April of the same year in Melitopol. A pogrom which took place in the provincial capital of Zhitomir surpassed all these in scope (May 1905). However, the severest pogroms of this period took place during the first week of November 1905, immediately after the publication of the manifesto of the czar (October 1905), which promised the inhabitants of Russia civic liberties and the establishment of a state Duma (Parliament). On publication of the manifesto, spontaneous manifestations of joy broke out throughout Russia. The celebrants came from the liberal and radical elements of Russian society, while the Jews, who hoped to obtain rapid emancipation, prominently participated in this rejoicing. In response to these manifestations, the reactionary circles organized popular processions of elements loyal to the regime; these were headed by the local civil and ecclesiastical leaders. In many places these processions developed into pogroms against the Jews (on some occasions, the non-Jewish intelligentsia was also attacked).

The most serious pogrom occurred in Odessa (with over 300 dead and thousands of wounded); another severe pogrom took place in Yekaterinoslav, where 120 Jews lost their lives. Altogether, pogroms were perpetrated in 64 towns (including, in addition to Odessa and Yekaterinoslav, Kiev, Kishinev, Simferopol, Romny, Kremenchug, Nikolayev, Chernigov, Kamenets-Podolski, and Yelizavetgrad), and 626 townlets and villages. About 660 of the pogroms took place in the Ukraine and Bessarabia, 24 outside the Pale of Settlement, and only seven in Belorussia.

Funeral for a member of the Socialist Zionist Party of Odessa, killed in the pogrom of 1905. Courtesy A. Raphaeli-Zenziper, Archive for Russian Zionism, Tel Aviv.

There were no pogroms in Poland and Lithuania. The total number of dead in these pogroms was estimated at over 800. The pogroms lasted only a few days. The most prominent participants were railway workers, small shop-keepers and craftsmen, and industrial workers. The peasants mainly joined in to loot property.

From the outset, these pogroms were inspired by government circles. The local authorities received instructions to give the pogromists a free hand and to protect them from the Jewish self-defense. Commissions of inquiry were appointed after the pogroms which explicitly pointed out the criminal inactivity of the police and military forces. After a while, it became known that pamphlets calling for the pogroms had been printed on the press of the governmental secret police.

Two further pogroms occurred in 1906. The first took place in Bialystok in June. About 80 Jews lost their lives and the mob looted and murdered under the protection of the military and police forces, who systematically opened fire on the Jews. This pogrom occurred during the session of the first Duma, which sent a commission of inquiry to

Bialystok. It also held a debate, in which direct responsibility for the pogrom was placed on the authorities. The second took place in Siedlce in August and was directly perpetrated by the police and military forces. About 30 Jews were killed and 180 wounded. With the suppression of the first Russian revolution, the pogroms were brought to a halt until the downfall of the old regime in 1917.

The pogroms of 1903–06 stimulated a great nationalist awakening among the Jews of Europe, they encouraged the development of organized self-defense movements among Jews, and greatly accelerated Jewish emigration to Erez Israel and the formation of the Hashomer [45] society in Erez Israel.

1917 to 1921. The third wave of pogroms occurred during the years 1917–21, in scope and gravity far surpassing the two previous outbreaks. These attacks on the Jews were connected with the revolutions and the civil war which took place in Eastern Europe during this period. At the end of 1917, pogroms had already occurred in the townlets and towns within proximity of the war front. The riot was headed by groups of soldiers from the disintegrating czarist army, and consisted of unruly acts against Jews by drunkards and of looting. Many pogroms of this type occurred in the Ukraine after the declaration of its independence in 1918. The first pogroms to be accompanied by slaughter of Jews were, however, perpetrated by units of the Red Army which retreated from the Ukraine in the spring of 1918 before the German army. These pogroms took place under the slogan of "Strike at the bourgeoisie and the Jews." The communities of Novgorod-Severski and Glukhov in northern Ukraine were the most severely affected. After a short period of confusion, the Soviets adopted stringent measures against pogromists found in the ranks of the Red Army. In addition to a fundamental and comprehensive information campaign, severe penalities

---

[45] Association of Jewish watchmen in Erez Israel which was active between 1909 and 1920

were imposed not only on guilty individuals who were executed but also on complete army units which were disbanded after their men had attacked Jews. Even though pogroms were still perpetrated after this, mainly by Ukrainian units of the Red Army at the time of its retreat from Poland (1920), in general, the Jews regarded the units of the Red Army as the only force which was able and willing to defend them.

In the spring of 1919, at the time of the retreat of the Ukrainian Army before the Red Army which occupied Kiev, units of the Ukrainian Army carried out organized military pogroms in Berdichev, Zhitomir, and other towns. These pogroms reached their climax in the massacre at Proskurov on Feb. 15, 1919, when 1,700 Jews were done to death within a few hours. On the following day, a further 600 victims fell in the neighboring townlet of Felshtin (Gvardeiskoye). Those responsible for these pogroms went unpunished, and henceforward the Ukrainian soldiers considered themselves free to spill Jewish blood. The Jews regarded Simon Petlyura, the prime minister of the Ukraine and commander of its forces, as responsible for these pogroms (in 1926 he was assassinated while in exile in Paris by Shalom Schwarzbard). The general chaos which reigned in the Ukraine in 1919 resulted in the formation of large and small bands of peasants who fought against the Red Army. The commanders of these bands (atamans) occasionally gained control of whole regions. The Jews in the villages, townlets, and towns there were constantly terrorized by the peasants, who extorted money ("contributions") and supplies from them or robbed and murdered them. These atamans included Angell, Kazakov, Kozyr-Zyrko, Struk, Volynets, Zeleny, Tutunik, and Shepel. The ataman Grigoryev, who in May 1919 seceded from the Red Army with his men, was responsible for pogroms in 40 communities and the deaths of about 6,000 Jews in the summer of 1919. He was killed by ataman Makhno, who led a peasant rebellion in eastern Ukraine and endeavored to restrain his men from attacking the Jews. One of the most notorious pogroms carried out by the peasant bands was that in Trostyanets in May 1919, when over 400 people lost their lives.

In the fall of 1919, there was a wave of pogroms in the wake of the counterrevolutionary "White Army," under the command of General A. I. Denikin, in its advance from northern Caucasus into the heart of Russia. This army, which sought to restore the ancient regime, proclaimed the slogan: "Strike at the Jews and save Russia." Its officers and soldiers made savage attacks on the Jews in every place which they occupied. The most sinister of these pogroms was in Fastov at the beginning of September 1919, in which about 1,500 Jewish men, women, and children were massacred. The soldiers of the "White Army" also perpetrated similar pogroms in other regions of Russia: in Siberia, where they were led by Admiral Kolchak and where the Cossack battalions of Baron R. Ungern-Sternberg gained notoriety for the systematic destruction of many communities in eastern Siberia and Mongolia; and in Belorussia, where Bulak-Balachowicz was in command in 1920. During 1920–21, when the Red Army gained control of Ukraine, the armed anti-Soviet bands still retained their full strength and the pogroms and brutalities against the Jews assumed a character of revenge, such as the massacre in Tetiev, in which about 4,000 Jews were put to death and the whole townlet was set on fire. The anti-Jewish movement set the total annihilation of the Jews as its objective and destroyed whole townlets. Only the military weakness of the attackers prevented a holocaust of Ukrainian Jewry.

During this period of pogroms, Jewish self-defense organizations were formed in many places throughout the Ukraine. The "Jewish Militia for War against Pogroms" of Odessa was renowned; it prevented pogroms in the largest community of Ukraine. Such groups were created in many towns and townlets but they were not always capable of withstanding military units or large armed bands. It was only after the consolidation of the Soviet regime that they 133 received its support and played an important role in the suppression of the armed bands movement.

It is difficult to assess the scope of the pogroms during the civil war years and the number of victims they claimed. Partial data are available for 530 communities in which 887 major pogroms and 349 minor pogroms occurred; there were 60,000 dead and several times that number of wounded. The pogroms which occurred in the years 1917–21 shocked East European Jewry, as well as world Jewry. On the one hand, they rallied many Jews to the Red Army and the Soviet regime; on the other, they strengthened the desire for the creation of a homeland for the Jewish people and a powerful and independent Jewish force.

9 PROTOCOLS OF THE ELDERS OF ZION

The specter of a worldwide Jewish conspiracy aiming at reducing the gentiles to slavery or exterminating them which loomed up in the Medieval Christian imagination, grew out of legends about well-poisoning and plague-spreading. Some such stories claimed that a secret rabbinical conference had been held to work out a detailed plan for ritual genocide of the Christians. From the time of the Renaissance, at first in Spain, these legends turned on a political plot rather than a religious one; similar notions circulated in France and Germany, after Napoleon's convocation of the Great Sanhedrin during February – March 1807. They did not gain widespread popular credence, nor at first did the versions launched during the second half of the century by French Catholic authors like Barruel and Bailly, who associated Freemasons and Jews in an anti-Christian plot. In its latest version, the legend of the "Elders of Zion" was concocted in Paris in the last decade of the 19th century by an unknown author working for the Russian secret police *(Okhrana)*; in all probability, it was intended to influence the policy of Czar Nicholas II toward the interests of the secret police. For his purposes, the anonymous forger adapted an old French political pamphlet by Maurice Joly attributing ambitions of world domination to Napoleon III, *Dialogue aux Enfers entre Machiavel et Montesquieu, ou la politique de Machiavel au xixe siècle* (1864), which does not have any allusions to Jews or Judaism. This "dialogue" was transformed into the "protocols" of an alleged conference of the leaders of world Jewry, who stated in summing up that, under the cloak of modern democracy, they already controlled the policies of numerous European states and were therefore very close to their objective. However the calculations of the Russian police misfired on that occasion: Nicholas II, impressionable and anti-Semitic though he was, detected the fraud, writing "One does not defend a worthy cause by vile means" in the margin of the manuscript submitted to him. The first Russian public edition of the *Protocols,* which appeared in 1905, did not attract much attention and was taken seriously in a few mystic and sectarian circles only.

The worldwide success of the *Protocols* dates from 1919 to 1921; after the widespread slaughter in World War I, the Russian Revolution in 1917, and the risings in Germany, many people felt impelled to discover a "hidden cause" for such tragic and momentous events. The text was widely circulated during the Russian civil war by propagandists seeking to incite the masses against the "Jewish Revolution," and undoubtedly contributed to the extensive pogroms perpetrated in southern Russia between 1918 and 1920. After the defeat of the White armies, Russian émigrés publicized the *Protocols* in the West. Translations followed, but most reputable European newspapers, such as *The Times* of London, questioned their authenticity. In 1921 the English journalist Philip Graves pointed out the close similarity between the text of the *Protocols* and Joly's pamphlet; from then on, balanced and responsible circles refused to take them seriously. This was no bar to an enormous circulation of the text, which was translated into all the main world languages. In the United States it was even sponsored (until 1927) by the influential and popular Henry Ford I.

However, well before the Nazi rise to power, the *Protocols* found the largest number of adherents in Germany. The theory of the occult power of the Jews, sworn enemies of German-Christian culture, perfectly suited those reactionary propagandists who attributed Germany's defeat to "a stab in the back." Right from the start the Nazi Party propagated this theme. The Weltdienst

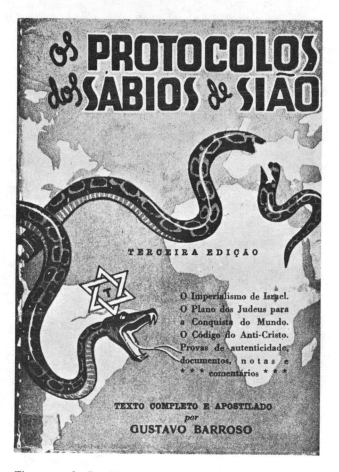

The cover of a Brazilian edition of the *Protocols*, 1937.

organization of Erfurt was specially formed to diffuse it and
to strengthen ties with anti-Semites in other countries. In
Berne in 1934 the Jewish community of Switzerland
brought the distributors of the *Protocols* to trial, establishing in court that the work was a forgery, but this did **137**

nothing to diminish the zeal of its propagators. During World War II, the *Protocols of the Learned Elders of Zion* became an implicit justification for the genocide of the Jews; and Nazi propaganda relied on them until the last days of the Third Reich. Although since 1945 no more than bibliographical curiosity in the majority of civilized countries, the *Protocols* have been reissued in numerous Arab states and President Nasser of Egypt publicly vouched for their authenticity. A Spanish edition, published in 1963, was probably an attempt to prevent the revision of the Catholic Church's traditional attitude toward the Jews at the Ecumenical Council Vatican II.

10 ANTI-SEMITIC POLITICAL PARTIES AND ORGANIZATIONS

A definite distinction must be made between organizations that temporarily adopted anti-Semitic attitudes and those founded with the express purpose of fighting "Jewish influences." Into the first category fall some originally liberal groups, especially in Austria and Rumania, as well as most of the clerical parties. For example, the German Catholic Center Party blamed Bismarck's *Kulturkampf* on the Jews but later relented and even protected Jewish religious interests. Many conservative groups vacillated in a similar fashion as did certain socialist movements, like the Fourierists in France, some disciples of F. Lassalle in Germany, and the Narodniki in Russia. Even the later united strong Social-Democrat parties rid themselves rather tardily of anti-Semitic tendencies. However the groups that called themselves "Christian-Social" were steeped in anti-Semitism, although for some of them anti-Judaism served mainly as a means of vote-catching and of competing with all-round anti-Semitic parties, while for others it constituted an integral part of their program.

The appearance of anti-Jewish parties and organizations, whether they were based on economic, religious, or *voelkisch* ("national-racist") ideologies or a combination of all three, constitutes the most important distinguishing mark of modern anti-Semitism, which came to the fore after the political reshuffle of Europe following the wars of 1866 and 1870–71, and particularly after the general economic crisis of 1873. All anti-Semitic organizations aspired to influence public life by means of mass movements and parliamentary pressure groups. Although before World

War I most of them were shortlived and failed to acquire mass support, they registered local victories and accumulated valuable political experience. Moreover, by their incessant propaganda they infected large parts of the population with a latent anti-Semitism. Germany and Austria were the first countries to experience organized anti-Semitism, preceding Hungary and Poland. France on the one hand, and Russia and Rumania on the other, constitute separate categories.

Germany. In the mid-1870s certain anti-Semitic social reform groups of artisans, small traders, and clerks began to form local organizations. A prominent instance in Saxony was Ernst Schmeitzner's Society for the Protection of Artisans and Traders. Rural advocates of social reform also gathered in small societies. Groups like the Anti-Semitic League of Wilhelm Marr (1879) occupied themselves less with economic reform than with *voelkisch* issues. Thus, from the outset of organizational activities, two main trends in political anti-Semitism asserted themselves: the social and the racist trends. It must be added, however, that both were complex: there was a radical and a conservative trend in the reform associations, as well as rather radical and ultraconservative wings in the racist groups. This divergence caused incessant splits and re-formations in political anti-Semitism, rendering it more or less ineffective until the end of World War I.

The first political organizer to use anti-Semitism as a lever for a mass movement was the court preacher Adolf Stoecker in Berlin. Stoecker failed to attract followers to his Christian Socialist Workers' Party (1878) on a platform of Christian ethics and reconciliation between state and workers through state intervention in economics. In 1879, however, he hit upon anti-Semitism as a vote-catcher for artisans and other members of the lower-middle classes in his speech "Our Demands on Modern Judaism." His activities inspired the founding of the anti-Semitic students' movement, Verein Deutscher Studenten (1881). This was

not powerful in itself, but it imbued the old students'

organizations—the Corps and the Deutsche Burschens-chaft—with the spirit of racial intolerance, so that finally they excluded all Jews from membership. Meanwhile, Stoecker was elected, with Conservative help, to the Prussian Diet (1879) and to the Reichstag. Stoecker's initial success was paralleled in Saxony, where the First International Anti-Jewish Congress convened in Dresden in 1882, assembling under the shadow of the blood libel of Tisza-Eszlar, convened delegates from Germany, Austria, and Hungary. A standing committee decided on the founding of an Alliance Anti-Juive Universelle (an allusion to the Alliance Israélite Universelle),[46] and fixed a second congress to be held the following year in Chemnitz. This congress attracted additional delegates from Russia, Rumania, Serbia, and France, but no lasting unity was established. Later anti-Semitic congresses (Kassel 1886, Bochum 1889) were strictly German, and they too accomplished nothing.

During 1880 and 1881, some of Stoecker's most vociferous racist allies broke away. The first was Ernst Henrici, who headed a radical anti-conservative Soziale Reichspartei for about three years. Next was the ultraconservative Liebermann von Sonnenberg, who in conjunction with Friedrich Nietzsche's brother-in-law, Bernhard Foerster, established the Deutscher Volksverein (1881–83). Both parties remained weak, and their endeavors to win general support by presenting to Bismarck their joint anti-Semitic petition asking for the abolition of Jewish equality gained them only fleeting success. Although they collected 225,000 signatures, they failed at the polls. When in 1883 the Conservative Party severed all connections with them, the center of political anti-Semitism shifted for a time from Berlin to small towns and rural districts and to other German states. This happened in 1886 when Theodor Fritsch of Leipzig, one of the most rabid racists, joined with the "Hessian King of Peasants," Otto Boeckel, and

[46] International Jewish organization, founded 1860, centered in Paris

others in the Deutsche Antisemitische Vereinigung. Boeckel was immediately elected to the Reichstag as the first anti-Semite per se. Before the elections of 1890 he founded his own Anti-Semitic People's Party (renamed in 1893 Deutsche Reformpartei), enjoying a certain measure of cooperation with Liebermann von Sonnenberg's reshuffled Deutschsoziale Partei. Thus in 1890 von Sonnenberg, Boeckel, and three of Boeckel's followers were elected to the Reichstag, the latter forming the first anti-Semitic parliamentary group. The 1893 elections showed even more striking gains: 16 anti-Semitic candidates were elected, half of them in Hesse.

This increase was brought about by the general political constellation, by a definite anti-Semitic turn in the Conservative Party, which adopted an openly anti-Jewish paragraph in its so-called Tivoli Program (1892), and by the entrance of the feudal-agrarian Bund der Landwirte ("Agrarian League") into the political arena as an ultraconservative and anti-Semitic pressure group. Finally, there emerged in Berlin a new rabble-rouser, Hermann Ahlwardt, the "headmaster of all the Germans." Ahlwardt's triumphs were, however, shortlived. In 1894 he was received into the parliamentary faction of the now-united wings of Liebermann, von Sonnenberg, and Boeckel, the Deutschsoziale Reformpartei (D.S.R.P.), but was soon excluded again. Boeckel himself lost his seat in 1903 to a candidate from a Protestant group. Nevertheless, 11 anti-Semites were elected in 1903, and three more joined them at by-elections. However, the realignments within their ranks continued. Von Sonnenberg's Deutschsoziale joined forces with the Agrarian League, the Christian-Socialists, and the Bavarian Peasant Party. Thus a parliamentary alignment, Wirtschaftliche Vereinigung, was established. Only the remnants of the D.S.R.P. held aloof, commanding six seats in 1907 and three in 1912, while the Wirtschaftliche Vereinigung secured 19 and ten respectively. On the eve of World War I, although again amalgamated into a Deutschvoelkische Partei (1914), party anti-Semitism seemed to be declining, but other previously non-anti-Semitic groups had been deeply infected by its vociferous activities. Even the left-wing liberal parties (alternately called Fortschritt, Freisinn, and again Fortschritt), which had staunchly defended Jewish equality, began making election agreements with anti-Semites or otherwise alienating their Jewish followers. It was therefore not surprising that various club-like right-wing groups openly pursued an anti-Jewish line. Such groups, mostly pan-Germanic and imperialist in outlook, comprised beside the already mentioned Students' and Agrarian Leagues, the Akademischer Turnerbund (from 1883), other gymnastic clubs imbued with Friedrich Ludwig Jahn's [47] exclusive nationalism, the Alldeutscher Verband ("Pan-Germanic League"), a small but effective organization of influential right-wing personalities, the somewhat similar Colonial Society, and many others. Of another hue was the Deutschnationaler Handlungsgehilfenverband—D.H.V. (from 1893), which became Germany's largest white-collar union, combining trade-union activities with conservative nationalist and anti-Semitic policies. In 1933 the D.H.V. merged with the Nazis in the National Socialist labor front. Among the small, lodge-like organizations were the Deutschbund of Friedrich Lange (1894), the Deutsche Volksbund of Boeckel (1907), the Germanen und Waelsungenorden (1912), whose activities were coordinated with Fritsch's Reichs-Hammerbund, and many others.

Austria and the Hapsburg Dominions. Although there are many similarities in the development of the German and Austrian anti-Semitic organizations, there remain two main differences. Christian-Socialist anti-Semitism played a leading part in Catholic Austria and even included the conservatives, while in Germany Protestant conservatism never relinquished its predominance over the Christian-Social movement. Secondly, "pure" racial anti-Semitism in

[47] German educator, publicist, and father of gymnastics (or Turnvater), died in 1852

Austria partly derived from the liberal camp, because of the essentially German nationalism of Austrian liberalism which denied the various minorities the right of self-determination. Yet the minorities themselves were often anti-Semitic, regarding Jews as proponents of Hapsburg domination. On the other hand, pan-German racism antagonized the minorities and did not attain the same influence as in Germany. Chronologically, students' unions led the way, excluding Jews as early as 1878. Soon the first Societies for the Protection of the Artisans (from 1880) amalgamated in the Oesterreichischer Reformverein (1882), which, under the leadership of Franz Holubek, was temporarily the main anti-Semitic organization. Later also the Deutsche Schulverein, supporting German schools in non-German territories, excluded Jews (1896), as did the nationalist Turnverein, cycling clubs, and the Deutsch-Oesterreichischer Alpenverein, which, however, adopted anti-Semitism only at the end of World War I.

The way for anti-Semitism as a force in party politics was paved by Georg Ritter von Schoenerer, who gradually shifted from liberalism to the extreme nationalist pan-Germanic wing, his movement probably influencing the young Adolf Hitler. In 1888, when Von Schoenerer was sentenced to prison for assault, his Deutschnationaler Verein began to dissolve, and the road was clear for the ascendancy of the Christian-Social movement. Karl von Vogelsang was its ideological mainspring and Karl Lueger its leading personality. They first attached themselves to the Christlich-Sozialer Verein (founded in 1887). Lueger, although still associated with a Jew (Julius Mandl), gradually identified himself with a newly formed anti-Jewish and anti-liberal election alignment, the United Christians (from 1887). In Vienna he formed a special anti-Semitic city branch (Buergerklub), and in the Austrian Reichsrat he led the Free Union for Economic Reform on a Christian Basis. These Christian-Social organizations backed him for the mayoralty of Vienna, although the nationalist elements broke away and formed the shortlived Deutschnationale

Vereinigung (1896–1900). He also enlarged the Christian-Social field of action outside the capital by means of Peasant Unions; he was helped by an able organizer, Msgr. Joseph Scheicher. Thus, in the elections of 1902 all 51 anti-Semitic members of the lower Austrian Diet were Christian-Socialists.

Catholic conservatives (united since 1895 in the Catholic People's Party) also wanted Lueger; when the introduction of a general ballot in 1907 raised the number of Christian-Social members in the Reichsrat to 67, about 29 conservatives joined with them in a parliamentary *Klub,* thus establishing the Christian-Social movement as the protagonist of Austrian conservatism also. Only the radicals, continuing Von Schoenerer's pan-Germanic racism, went their separate way, mainly among the German elements in the Czech Sudetenland. Here the Deutsche Arbeiterpartei (1903, later called Deutsche Nationalsozialistische Arbeiterpartei) and the Deutsche Agrarpartei (1905), with their anticlerical, anti-Jewish, and anti-Czech attitude, registered considerable gains. However, anti-Semitism in the Hapsburg countries was not a German monopoly. Czech, Polish, and Ruthenian nationalists were sporadically as anti-Jewish as they were anti-German, or anti-Russian and anti-Polish, all regarding the Jews as part of rival nationalism, or decrying them as entirely foreign.

In Hungary. Győző Istóczy, from the liberal benches of the Diet, started local anti-Semitic cells, similar to Marr's Anti-Semitic League. He boasted that in 1880 there were already 78 such cells, which he hoped to amalgamate into a Union of Non-Jews. After the riots and pogroms which followed the Tisza-Eszlar blood libel, Istóczy and Simonyi, a "national-social" anti-Semite, founded the Anti-Semitic Club for the elections of 1884. They gained 17 seats and captured the majority in the Bratislava municipality, but quarreled among themselves and dissolved again. Later, Count Ferdinand Zichy's Christian-Social movement (Catholic People's Party, founded in 1895) attracted much anti-Semitic support, but was not to the taste of radical-nationalists, although it spread vicious anti-Jewish propaganda.

Poland. While anti-Semitism in Czechoslovakia and Hungary was more or less sporadic, it was endemic in Galicia and Russian Poland. Already in the 1880s it had found a spokesman in Teofil Merunowicz, who advocated anti-Jewish legislation in the Galician Diet. During the 1890s, the Polish Catholic People's Party, led by Jan Stapiński, which sponsored social measures like rural producers' and consumers' cooperatives, also supported anti-Jewish boycott measures. When the Jesuit Father Stojalowski took over the direction of propaganda, this Christian Social movement even initiated a wave of pogroms during the by-elections of 1898, in which Father Stojalowski was returned to the Diet. At the same time, the National Democratic Party (N.D.K., *Endeks*) organized the radical national forces, mainly in Russian Poland. The National Democrats and their propaganda were instrumental in transferring anti-Semitism into the new Polish state founded after World War I.

France. In the abovementioned countries, with the exception of Russian Poland, political anti-Semitism emerged as an immediate reaction to the granting of Jewish emancipation. French Jewry had already been emancipated for 80 years when it was hit by the organized forms of Jew-hatred. The chaotic conditions after the French defeat by Germany in 1871, the bloodbath of the Paris Commune, and the birth pangs of the unloved Third Republic formed the background for anti-liberalism, anti-parliamentarism, and anti-Semitism. Even socialists, influenced by the teachings of Fourier, Proudhon, and Toussenel, quickly adopted the image of Rothschild as the symbol of financial capitalism. But in the main, French feelings against the Jews, whether of a conservative or of a democratic and social type, were inspired by Catholicism. In its fight against liberalism and socialism Catholicism was looking for a scapegoat; this it found first in Freemasonry and finally in a "Jewish plot," allegedly exploiting the Masonic order to attain "world domination."

Paralleling Austrian developments, the French-Social-Catholic movement started in the 1870s with rather conservative Catholic Workers' Clubs; their anti-Semitism gradually increased, especially after the collapse of the Catholic bank Union Générale in 1882. However no mass organization emerged until about 1890, with the formation of the Christian Democratic movement by forces that took their inspiration from Edouard Drumont's book *La France Juive* (1886). Such a movement also served as a refuge for the disillusioned remnants of General Boulanger's supporters. Certain Boulangists and Boulangist organizations, like Paul Déroulède's Patriotic League, had already dabbled in anti-Semitism, as had Jacques de Biez, one of the first followers of Drumont, who in 1886 attended the founding ceremony of the Alliance Anti-Israélite Universelle in Bucharest It was only during the course of elections in 1890, however, that the French National Anti-Semitic League took shape, under the leadership of the Marquis de Morès and Jules Delahaye, as an election alignment for Boulangists and adherents of Drumont. It quickly disintegrated, its candidates being defeated at the polls. An attempt by Morès to organize the Paris street mob into strong-arm brigades did not help, but it invited imitations (see below). The Christian Democrats became more republican and radical, and most violently anti-Semitic during the Dreyfus Affair. Typical of this development are the utterances of the anti-monarchist Father Hippolyte Gayraud at the first Christian Democratic Congress in Lyons (1896). Gayraud held that the church had always been anti-Semitic "on a high moral plane," and that "all social excrement, especially the Jews" should be expelled from France. The movement quickly disintegrated after the pardon of Dreyfus in 1906. Meanwhile, however, anti-Semitism prospered, not only in Paris, but also in the provincial towns where anti-Semitic small businessmen's and salesmen's organizations sprang up in Lyons, Poitiers, Dijon, Nancy, and other places, and finally in Algiers, where Max

Régis instigated anti-Jewish atrocities, gaining for himself the mayoralty and for Drumont a seat in the Chamber of Deputies. In Paris itself, the most important local group before 1897, when Jules Guerin renewed the Ligue Antisémite and organized the mob into anti-Dreyfusard and anti-Jewish commandos, was the Students' Anti-Semitic League (1894), which remained active in the streets and at the university during the Dreyfus Affair. Several of its founders later formed a National Anti-Jewish Party (1901), but finally joined l'Action Française. This extreme chauvinist and royalist group (founded in 1899), which sponsored a conservative "landed anti-Semitism," remained a political force for more than 40 years, until Hitler's conquest of France.

Rumania. In Rumania and czarist Russia, anti-Semitism was to a large extent government-sponsored. In "constitutional" Rumania parliamentary parties flourished and vied among themselves in sponsoring anti-Jewish measures, turning parliament itself into the main stage for anti-Semitic propaganda and for discriminative legislation against the "foreigners," in flagrant violation of international commitment (see Congress of Berlin). In this, the so-called Liberal Party under John Bratianu surpassed the conservatives, as the land-owning boyars were to a certain extent interested in protecting "their" Jews. In 1886, under the influence of Edouard Drumont, Bucharest served as the center for a new departure in international anti-Semitism: the Alliance Anti-Israélite Universelle was founded by Rumanian, Hungarian, and French intransigents, Drumont being unanimously elected president. But this time, too, the international organization very quickly proved abortive. About ten years later (1895), the Rumanians organized their own Universal Anti-Semitic League with A. C. Cuza,[48] the deputy N. Jorga, and other members of parliament and high officials in leading positions. It established branches in many towns, pledging itself "to make life intolerable" for

---

[48] Rumanian nationalist and anti-Semitic leader (1857–1946)

Jews and to force them out of the country. In the following years pogroms in Rumania were numerous and vicious, culminating in rural anti-Jewish riots that led to a general peasant uprising, which in 1907 had to be quelled by the army. On the eve of World War I, the so-called "Culture-League" continued the pogrom propaganda in derision of its name, vowing to create a situation in which "Russia with its pogroms and blood libels would seem to be a Promised Land to the Jews."

Russia. Although Russia was the land of the most violent anti-Semitism, it had perhaps the fewest organizations devoted to it, for Russian autocratic patterns of government did not allow even anti-Semitic groups. Thus, the first known reactionary anti-Semitic organization, the Sacred League, which sprang up after the assassination of Czar Alexander II in March 1881, was clandestine, although arch-reactionary high officials and even ministers seem to have furthered it. In their eyes the Jews were the source of all rebellion, and they themselves used terror and violence to destroy the "leaven of revolution." It is generally believed that the Sacred League was instrumental in fomenting the pogroms of 1881 and 1882. It was dissolved at the end of that year. Toward the end of 1904, when the Japanese war was going badly for Russia, and early in 1905, when the revolution broke out, another anti-Semitic organization was formed, the Union of the Russian People, rather similar in character and aims to its predecessor. This league was openly recognized, and even furthered by the czar and his government, together with its secret fighting squads, the "Black Hundred," which were largely responsible for the pogroms of 1905 and for counterrevolutionary political assassinations. The Union of the Russian People, acting in the open, continued in existence until World War I, and inspired the formation of several similar "patriotic" organizations. Perhaps its most reactionary offspring was the United Nobility (1911), one of its leading spirits being N. E. Markov. This party openly advocated the complete expulsion of the Jews from the country, and did much to spread blood libels against the Jews which finally culminated in the Beilis case. Even during the war, government-sponsored anti-Semitism scarcely abated and was responsible for the allegation of an act of Jewish high treason against the Russian Army in the village of Kuzhi (1915), which was given wide publicity by every Russian newspaper.

11 ANTI-JEWISH BOYCOTTS

Anti-Jewish boycott pressure has to a large extent accompanied anti-Semitism as one of its more dangerous and frequent manifestations. Contacts with Jews were avoided, Jews were not accepted in merchants' guilds, trade associations, and similar organizations. This form of boycott often coincided with legal and administrative restrictions already in force in the country.

Toward the late end of the 19th century, the anti-Jewish boycott became one of the basic weapons used for victimizing the Jewish population. The first International Anti-Jewish Congress in Dresden, 1882 (see above, Anti-Semitic Political Parties and Organizations), adopted a slogan against Jewish merchants and professionals. In Western Europe, the boycott took the form of excluding Jews from membership of certain societies. In Eastern Europe the rapidly developing "national" bourgeoisie, which formed the mainstay of the rightist parties, soon adopted anti-Semitic tactics in the effort to squeeze out Jewish competitors. The anti-Jewish boycott campaign met with success in many parts of the Austro-Hungarian Empire. The Austrian anti-Semites publicized in the press and at public meetings the slogan, "Don't buy from Jews." When the government declared this slogan illegal, it was changed into "Buy from Christians only." In Bohemia and Moravia the anti-Jewish boycott spread under the slogan "Each to his own" *(svůj k svému),* at a time when the rising bourgeoisie sought to obtain an exclusive position in the economy, especially in trade.

Shortly before World War I the Ukrainian population of Galicia was swept into a boycott movement instigated because of alleged Jewish collaboration with the Poles. At the same time, some Polish public figures in Galicia (for instance, the priest Stojalkowski) proposed the boycott as a form of defense for the Polish population against alleged Jewish exploitation. In Russia, the boycott did not attain significant proportions, despite the strongly nationalist and anti-Jewish stand of the Russian merchants. The system of legal and administrative restrictions against the Jews already operating in Czarist Russia was more efficient than any form of boycott. A similar situation existed in Rumania, where the Jews had been deprived of all rights of citizenship and were considered "foreigners" in the legal sense. They were not allowed to practice the liberal professions, or keep tobacconist shops (which were a state monopoly), pharmacies, etc. Following the Russian example, Rumania introduced the *numerus clausus* in educational institutions. Jewish factory owners were obliged by law to employ two-thirds non-Jewish workers. In 1907 "foreigners" were prohibited from holding agricultural farms on lease. The anti-Jewish boycott drive was especially intensive in Polish areas, which at that time did not form a national state. The newspaper *Rola,* which began publication in the 1880s, proposed the slogan of "Polonization" of trade and industry. Developments took a decisive turn in the following decade when the National Democratic Party (*Narodowa Demokracja, N.D.K.* "Endeks"), led by Roman Dmowski, appeared on the political horizon. Initially the Endeks did not come out with anti-Semitic slogans and confined their campaign to the "Litvaks," Jews from Russia, whom they accused of promoting the Russification of Poland.

The crushing of the 1905–07 revolution in Russia was also a major setback to the aspirations of the Polish community for political liberation, and it now began to interest itself exclusively in economic problems. The Endek party campaigns became increasingly aggressive, adopting the slogans "Each to his own," "Don't buy Jewish," and "Buy Christian only." The boycott also spread to cultural life, giving birth to numerous exclusively "Catholic" or "Christian" organizations. The anti-Jewish boycott received wide public support after 1912 in connection with the elections for the Fourth Russian Duma. The Jewish voters did not support the candidate put up by the rightist Polish party, and their votes secured the election of the Socialist candidate. In retaliation the rightist press started an intensive anti-Jewish campaign, proclaiming the beginning of the "Polish-Jewish War." The boycott in Polish areas appears to have been coordinated with the anti-Semitic campaign simultaneously unleashed in Russia in connection with the Beilis case.

Between the two world wars anti-Jewish boycott agitation continued particularly in Poland where the situation deteriorated in the wake of economic difficulties, especially following the depression. In an endeavor to soft-pedal the rising social tension, rightist anti-Semitic circles, with the silent approval of the authorities, pointed

Nazi pickets outside a German Jewish shop. The placard says, "Germans! Defend yourselves! Don't buy from Jews!"

A 1933 poster warns Berliners to "avoid Jewish doctors and lawyers." Jerusalem, Yad Vashem Archives.

at the Jews as the cause of the distress of millions of unemployed. Taking over trade from the Jews was made to serve as a panacea for rampant poverty and unemployment. After the Nazi rise to power in Germany the government publicly announced a general anti-Jewish boycott. Nazi agitators urged boycotting the Jews at mass meetings. On Saturday, April 1, 1933, uniformed Nazi pickets appeared in front of Jewish shops, attacked their clients, and wrote anti-Jewish slogans on their windows. The offices of Jewish doctors, lawyers, and engineers were also picketed. The official German policy roused anti-Semitic circles in neighboring countries to more extreme action. The anti-Jewish boycott in Poland gathered strength in imitation of the Nazi example, and Polish anti-Semitic groups began to adopt active boycott pressure. Pickets appeared in front of Jewish shops and stalls and terrorized the Jewish merchants as well as their non-Jewish clients. The rising number of incidents sometimes resulted in the destruction of shops and goods and also an occasional bloody pogrom, as at Przytyk and Wysokie Mazowieckei.

Anti-Jewish boycott activities received the stamp of official approval in 1937, when Prime Minister Slawoj-Skladkowski let drop in his notorious statement the slogan "economic boycott?—please!" The Polish government also attempted to step up Jewish emigration from Poland by means of economic strangulation. The boycott did not greatly affect Jewish industrialists and big businessmen, with whom the most rabid propagandists of the anti-Jewish boycott movement not infrequently had secret commercial ties. However, it weighed heavily on hundreds of thousands of small businessmen, artisans, and others. The anti-Jewish boycott—frequently referred to as the "cold pogrom" in the inter-war press—undermined the foundations of the livelihood of hundreds of thousands of Jews.

12 NUMERUS CLAUSUS

Numerus Clausus i.e. "closed number" is an amount fixed as maximal number in the admission of persons (or certain groups of persons) to specific professions (in particular the liberal professions), institutions of higher learning, professional associations, positions of public office, etc. It is frequently applied to Jews. Numerus clausus on the admission of Jews to institutions of higher learning was applied in the 19th century, and extended in the 20th century, in particular in the countries of Eastern Europe, but also in others. It assumed its most characteristic form in czarist Russia (see below) as the *protsentnaya norma* where the restrictions and limitations on the admission of Jews were established by special legislation. In countries such as Poland and Rumania (see below) the numerus clausus was introduced as a quasi-legal means, or was applied in practice, as part of an anti-Semitic policy. However, in democratic countries the numerus clausus was also tacitly applied, at least in some institutions of higher learning, for social or prestige reasons. A numerus clausus of this type was applied not only to students but also (sometimes principally) to teaching staff in the universities or in admission to the civil or public services where higher professional qualifications were required. It was also applied in admission to positions which carried a special status, as in the higher ranks of the civil service, the diplomatic service, army, etc.

In Czarist Russia. During the first half of the 19th century, the policy of the Russian government toward the Jews, as formulated in the statutes concerning the Jews *("polozheniya")* of 1804, 1835, and 1844, was to attract the Jewish youth to Russian schools. This ambition encountered strong opposition from the Jewish masses who regarded education in these schools as a step toward the alienation of Jewish youth from its people and its religion. They also viewed the network of Jewish state schools established by the government to promote general education among the Jews with suspicion. In 1853 there were 159 Jewish pupils in all the secondary schools of Russia (1.3% of the total student roll), while in the universities there were a few dozen. On the other hand, the *maskilim* advocated education in the Russian schools as a means of rapprochement with the Russian people.

During the reign of Alexander II, a radical change occurred in the attitude of the Jews, especially those of the middle and upper classes, toward the Russian schools. This was due to the privileges granted to educated Jews (extension of the right of residence in 1865; important concessions with regard to military service in 1874). In 1880 the number of Jewish pupils in the secondary schools rose to 8,000 (11.5% of the total) and in the universities to 556 (6.8% of the total). These numbers increased yearly. In the educational region of Odessa (which included southern Russia) the proportion of Jewish students rose to 35.2%, and in the region of Vilna (Lithuania) to 26.7%. A Russian-Jewish stratum of intelligentsia rapidly became prominent. As service in the government and administration was closed to them, this intelligentsia concentrated in the liberal professions—medicine, law, and journalism. The members of these professions soon became aware of growing competition from Jews. A propaganda campaign was instigated against the admission of Jews into the class of the intelligentsia; this was sparked off in 1880 by a letter to the editor entitled *Zhid Idyot* ("The Jew is Coming") which was published in the widely influential newspaper *Novoye Vremya*.

Of their own initiative, higher and secondary schools in various parts of the country began to restrict the admission of Jews within their precincts. This coincided with the general policy of the government of Alexander III which 157 sought to prevent the admission of children of the poorer classes into the higher and secondary schools. It was claimed that the Jewish students introduced a spirit of rebellion and revolution into the schools and thus had a deleterious influence over their Christian fellow students. In July 1887 the Ministry of Education decided that the proportion of Jews in all secondary schools and higher institutions subject to its jurisdiction was not to surpass 10% in the towns of the Pale of Settlement, 5% in the towns outside it, and only 3% in the capitals of St. Petersburg and Moscow. Many schools were completely closed to Jews. In time, this regulation also spread to schools which were under the supervision of other government ministries (ministry of communications, ministry of finance, etc.). There were individual cases, after the Revolution of 1905, where the restrictions and admission prohibitions were also applied to converted Jews.

These restrictions were introduced during a period when masses of Jewish youth were besieging the Russian schools, and had severe repercussions on Jewish life. Only those who had obtained the highest marks and distinctions were likely to be admitted to Russian secondary and high schools. There were naturally instances of bribery and corruption, or parents who baptized their children so that they could enter the schools. Secondary school graduates began to convert for this end, and during the years 1907 to 1914 this became commonplace. The Lutheran clergyman Piro of Finland became known for selling baptismal certificates at a low price to all those who desired them *("pirovtsy")*. The Jewish national and Zionist movements fought this phenomenon. These regulations also resulted in the emigration of thousands of Jewish youths to study at the universities of Western Europe (Switzerland, Germany, France, etc.). Jewish students formed the majority of the "Russian" colonies in the university towns of the West. In 1892 the number of Jewish pupils in the secondary schools had decreased to 5,394 (7% of the pupils).

158   Jewish youths took advantage of the possibility of

completing their studies by means of external examinations. In Jewish society, the "extern" made his appearance, who studied under the guidance of private teachers and then sat for the state examinations. The anti-Semitic examiners were severe and failed many of them. In 1911 it was decided that the numerus clausus would also apply to external students, and since the number of non-Jewish external students was very limited this system was brought to an end. During the period of the Russian Revolution of 1905, when autonomy was granted to the institutions of higher learning, the numerus clausus was abolished, but immediately upon the repression of the Revolution the practice was restored. The proportion, however, was increased (to 15% in the Pale of Settlement, 10% beyond it, and 5% in the capital cities). Accordingly, the number of Jewish pupils in the secondary schools rose to 17,538 (9.1% of the pupils), and of Jewish students at the universities to 3,602 (9.4%). In the overwhelming majority of secondary schools for girls, the numerus clausus was not introduced. In 1911 about 35,000 Jewish girls studied at Russian secondary schools (13.5% of the pupils). In the educational region of Vilna (Lithuania) the proportion of Jewish girl pupils rose to 49%, in the region of Warsaw to 42.7% and in the regions of Kiev and Odessa to 33.3% (these four educational regions encompassed the whole of the Pale of Settlement). The numerus clausus served as an impetus for the establishment of private Jewish secondary schools, several of which evolved the beginnings of a national Jewish education.

All restrictions on the admission of Jews to the secondary schools and institutions of higher learning were abolished with the Revolution of February 1917. In 1919, during the brief period when the armies of Denikin (the "White Army") gained control of large regions of southern Russia, the numerus clausus was temporarily reinstated in many towns under their control.

In the Soviet Union. There are no indications of any official or unofficial numerus clausus existing in the Soviet Union until the last "Black Years" of Stalin's rule 159

(1948–53). Even then discrimination against Jews seeking admission to Soviet universities seems to have been related to the general atmosphere of distrust and enmity, engendered by the anti-Jewish trend of official policy, rather than the result of a regulated system of limited percentages. Though legally and openly there has never been a numerus clausus for Jews in the U.S.S.R., young Jews seeking admission to certain prestige universities, or to studies leading to positions entailing use of classified information or representative status in the state or on its behalf, increasingly encountered unexpected artificial difficulties in the 1950s and 1960s. Many young Jews complained of having been rejected despite brilliant achievements in the entrance examinations in favor of non-Jews with fewer scholastic qualifications. A number of statements were made by Prime Minister Nikita Khrushchev (for instance to a French socialist delegation in 1957; see *Réalités,* May 1957) or by the minister of culture, Yekaterina Furtseva (to a correspondent of the pro-Communist American magazine, *National Guardian,* June 25, 1956) confirming the existence of a general policy to regulate cadres according to nationality—particularly and explicitly by reducing the proportion of Jews in the intelligentsia and in government departments. These statements seemed to validate the assumption of many Soviet citizens as well as of scholars abroad that, as W. Korey affirms in his study on the legal position of Soviet Jewry (1970), "unpublished governmental regulations appear to have been issued, whether in written or oral form, which establish quotas limiting educational or employment opportunities for Jews." In 1959 the minister for higher education, U. P. Yelyutin, vehemently denied the existence of such quotas, and in 1962 the U.S.S.R. ratified the UNESCO Convention against Discrimination in Education. However, some evidence to the contrary was found in 1963 in Soviet journals such as *Kommunist* and, particularly, the "Bulletin of Higher Education," which acknowledged the existence of "annually planned preferential admission quotas." An American specialist on Soviet education, N. de Witt, reached the conclusion in 1961 that a quota system existed "to the severe disadvantage of the Jewish population." According to de Witt the principle applied makes "the representation of any national or ethnic grouping in overall higher education enrollment" proportional to its size in the total Soviet population. He presented statistical data which showed that between 1935 and 1958 "the index of representation (in higher education) rose for most nationalities, but fell for Georgians and all national minorities, with a very drastic decline for the Jews."

The official statistics on the number of Jewish students, which apparently contradicted this assertion, were misleading (as some scholars, like Alec Nove and J. A. Newth, have found after a meticulous analysis, published in 1970), mainly because these overall numbers included not only students in every kind of "institute" and field of study, but also external (i.e., correspondence) students. The question whether Jews were "able to get into universities of their choice on equal terms with competitors of other nationalities" remained open. The percentage of Jewish students (including evening and correspondence students) fell from 14.4% in 1928–29 to 3.2% in 1960–61. Though the official percentage of Jews in the total population was in 1960–61 approximately 1.1% and in the urban population 2.2%, the above-mentioned percentage of Jewish students should be considered, according to A. Nove and J. A. Newth, to be proportionately low.

The majority of the Jewish proletariat perished during the German invasion in World War II, and there seems to be no doubt that, as a purely urban element consisting of white-collar workers, professional men, engineers, scientists, and people occupied in retail trade "a much larger proportion of Jews than of other nationalities endeavors to obtain higher education. It is this fact that may well give rise to discrimination. Some officials may feel that it is wrong for Jews to be so overwhelmingly non-proletarian in their composition. Others, particularly in the national 161 republics, are concerned to provide special educational advantages for the relatively backward peoples of their own nationality." This conclusion of A. Nove and J. A. Newth seems to be borne out by a large number of case histories related by Soviet Jews themselves.

In Poland. The numerus clausus was one of the manifestations of the widespread anti-Semitism in Poland between the two world wars. The Polish government made use of the numerus clausus as a quasi-legal means to limit the number of Jewish students in the institutions of higher education to the minimum. The total number of students in Poland increased continuously between 1920 and 1935. From 34,266 students in 1921–22, it rose to 47,200 in 1935–36. In the same period both the number of Jewish students and their proportion in the total declined. In 1920–21 there were 8,526 Jewish students in Poland; in 1923–24 their number reached its peak figure of 9,579; but in 1935–36 their number dropped to 6,200, i.e., a decrease of about 35%. The proportion of Jewish students in the total number of students was 24.6% in 1921–22, 20% in 1928–29, and only 13.2% in 1935–36.

The results of the numerus clausus are especially instructive if the fluctuations in the number of Jewish students in the various faculties are noted. The most striking instance is the faculty of medicine. In 1923–24 there were still 1,402 Jewish medical students, forming 30.2% of the total. In 1926–27 their number dropped to 698 (18.6%), and in 1935–36 Jewish medical students formed only 13.8% of the total number. In the faculty of law their percentage in 1923–24 was 24.6%, while in 1935–36 it was only 12.5%. In the humanities the numbers for the corresponding years were 35.4% and 18.3%, and in the faculty of chemistry 25% and 12%. This tendency to a continuous decrease in the number of Jewish students in all faculties, especially in the professions of medicine, law, and engineering, was an outcome of the numerus clausus policy. It hindered the admission of Jewish students to the institutions of higher education, although the number of Jewish applicants increased in Poland and a growing number of Jewish youths wished to enter academic professions.

In Poland up to World War II there were 14 state institutions of higher education, and nine nongovernmental (e.g., the Catholic University in Lublin; commercial colleges in Warsaw, Cracow, Lvov, Lodz, etc.). Almost all of these institutions applied the numerus clausus as the leading criterion in admitting new students, though some applied it more strictly than others. In the University of Lvov, for instance, the Jewish students comprised 46.6% of the total number of students in 1921–22, while in 1930–31 (there are no statistical data for later years) they comprised only 31.9%; in the University of Warsaw the figures for the corresponding years were 31.4% and 23.8%; in the Warsaw Polytechnic 15.5% and 10.2%; in the Veterinary College in Lvov 13% and 5.4%; and in the Institute of Dentistry, 70.4% and 19.7%.

The proportion of females among Jewish students throughout this period was higher than that among non-Jewish students. The percentage of Jewish females was 33.3% in 1923–24 and 39% in 1930–31, while the numbers among non-Jews for these years were 15% and 26%. The authorities of the academic institutions were more willing to admit Jewish female students than Jewish males, since many left the universities before graduating. Another reason for not strictly applying the numerus clausus toward Jewish women was that the majority studied in the faculty of humanities (philosophy, history, literature), instead of the more demanding professions. Thus, for instance, in 1930–31, 50% of the male students studied law; 11% medicine; 16.4% philosophy; and 14.6% sciences, while 11% of the female students studied law; 3.4% medicine; 63.2% philosophy; and 1.7% sciences. In the last few years preceding World War II the authorities took even stronger discriminatory measures against the Jewish students. They introduced the system of "Jewish benches," which allocated special benches at the back of the auditoriums and classrooms to be used only by Jews. The Jewish students revolted against these regulations and refused to sit there. This frequently led to serious clashes in the universities, resulting in bloodshed and tragedy.

In Rumania. In Rumania in 1922 a numerus clausus of the admission of Jewish students was advocated by Rumanian students in the University of Cluj. These were members of the Association of Christian Students, founded by adherents of A. C. Cuza in Jassy earlier that year. It was adopted also by the students in the universites of Jassy, Bucharest, and Cernauti (Chernovtsy). December 10, the day of its announcement by the students in Cluj, was declared a holiday throughout Rumania by the students, who every year took the opportunity to attack Jewish students on that day. The numerus clausus in Rumania was not introduced by law. However, in practice the Christian students, by using force, prevented the Jewish students from regular studies. The position of the science and medical students was especially serious since they were prevented from using the laboratories, taking part in autopsies, etc. In the late 1920s Jewish students in this sphere were forced to go abroad, especially to France and Italy, in order to complete their studies.

At first the majority of teachers in the universities were opposed to the students' anti-Semitic activities, but with the rise of National Socialism in Germany many professors supported the numerus clausus movement. In 1933 special entrance examinations were introduced and Jewish candidates were deliberately failed. The few who were accepted were prevented by the Christian students from taking part in the studies, and in some faculties there were no Jewish students at all. Thus the numerus clausus became a numerus nullus. The Association of Christian Students was subsidized by all ministers of the interior throughout this period.

In 1935 the Rumanian statesmen A. Vaida-Voevod declared a "numerus valahicus," (a "Walachian numerus"), a disguised form of the numerus clausus. The head of the Orthodox Church in Rumania, the patriarch Miron Cristea, declared his support of the numerus valahicus in the Rumanian senate.

A law on the employment of Rumanian employees was passed in 1934, which fixed a proportion of 80% for Rumanian workers in every place of employment, and 50% for Rumanians in their management. This law was felt especially in the textile industry, banking, and commerce, where a large number of Jews was employed. Professional and trade unions, such as the lawyers', accountants', clerical workers', etc., began to evict the Jews from their membership and refused to accept new Jewish members.

At the beginning of the pro-Nazi regime of Ion Antonescu in 1940, all Jewish students were officially expelled from the schools and universities. This was also the fate of the Jewish workers in the private economic sector.

In Hungary. Restrictions affecting the admission of Jewish students into the institutions of higher learning in Hungary were passed as a law in 1920. This laid down that no new students should be accepted in the universities unless they were "loyal from the national and moral standpoint," and that "the proportion of members of the various ethnic and national groups in the total number of students should amount to the proportion of such ethnic and national groups in the total population." According to the official ground for this enactment, the law was intended to prevent a surplus of persons in the liberal professions, which the dismembered country was unable to integrate. But it was clear that the law was directed against the Jews only.

The leaders of the Neologists[49] in Hungarian Jewry who considered the law a severe blow to Jewish equal rights, as well as the liberal opposition and especially its Jewish representatives, attempted to combat the law, but without success. Jewish students who were not admitted to institutions of higher learning were forced to go abroad to study in Germany, Austria, Czechoslovakia, Italy, France, and Belgium. The Jewish students who were admitted despite the restrictions were often insulted and sometimes beaten up by the non-Jewish students, whose "ideal" was to achieve a "numerus nullus."

Outside Hungary a number of Jewish organizations initiated a struggle against the law on the international level in 1921, basing their claims on the peace treaty of Trianon, in which Hungary had guaranteed that all its citizens should "be equal before the law . . . without distinction of race, language, or religion." The Jewish organizations sent a petition based on these lines to the League of Nations. However, the official leadership of Hungarian Jewry refrained from cooperating with these Jewish organizations. Nevertheless the international Jewish organizations received support from Jews in Hungary as well as from the Hungarian Jewish students studying abroad.

The Hungarian government, when asked by the League of

[49] Neology (Neologism), unofficial name of the communities in Hungary belonging to the Reform movement

Nations to supply information concerning this question, avoided the issue by providing statistical data showing that the Jews were not discriminated against by this law. In 1925 the Joint Foreign Committee and the Alliance Israélite Universelle, fearing that other countries would adopt the numerus clausus, appealed to the Permanent Court of International Justice. This time Hungary was compelled to give a relevant answer. The Hungarian minister of education claimed in 1927 that the law was merely temporary, arising from Hungary's difficult situation, and undertook that the law would shortly be amended. When the amendment was not forthcoming Hungary was asked to hasten the procedure, and in 1928 the bill was submittd to the Hungarian parliament. According to this amendment racial criteria in admitting new students were removed and replaced by social criteria. Five categories were set up: civil servants, war veterans and army officers, small landowners and artisans, industrialists, and the merchant classes. The result was much the same. According to the new socioeconomic criteria the Jews had approximately the same status as before. The theoretically nonracial character of the amended law was a temptation to convert to Christianity. Indeed many Jews did so, like their predecessors of an earlier period, for the sake of office. The numerus clausus remained in force despite the protests of Jews and liberals.

By the second anti-Jewish law passed in 1939 the admission of new students was again put on a racial and not a confessional basis. Students of the rabbinical seminary were exempted from the law's application, since according to the government regulations of this institution its students required a doctorate in philosophy in order to obtain their rabbinical diploma, and were restricted in their choice of subject to oriental studies and philosophy. The Hungarian constituent national assembly which convened in Debrecen in December 1944 abolished the numerus clausus among the rest of the discriminatory racial legislation.

In the United States. In the United States mass immigration after 1881 resulted in the partial exclusion of Jews from many of the professions. There were very few Jews in the teaching profession before 1930. In 1920 there were 214 Jewish students in the medical schools of the State of New York; by 1940 there were only 108 in the same schools. In its Annual Report in 1932, the American Jewish

Committee was willing to accept the proposition that this

exclusion was not entirely due to anti-Semitism but that there was "overcrowding in an already overcrowded profession" and that Jews needed to be redirected to other pursuits. This was a vain hope in an era when the opportunities for Jews in the professions were constantly decreasing, so that, for example, the proportion of Jews in veterinary medicine decreased from almost 12% to less than 2% between 1935 and 1946. The situation was somewhat better in dentistry, where by the mid-1930s about one-fifth of the students in the dental schools were Jews, but even here the leaders of the profession tried to keep Jews out.

This trend of exclusion during most of the first half of the 20th century reached down into the undergraduate schools. There was a famous incident in 1923 when President Eliot of Harvard advised that the enrollment of Jews should be limited at his school, in order to preserve the representative character of the leading academic institution of the United States. The committee that he appointed at Harvard was unanimous in opposing him and in insisting that places be given to applicants solely on the basis of merit. Eliot was denounced by the American Federation of Labor, the Boston city council, and the legislature of the State of Massachusetts, which body threatened to remove the tax exemptions that Harvard enjoyed if a discriminatory policy were followed. Despite the storm an unofficial numerus clausus continued until after World War II in most of the major American colleges and universities. In 1931 Rutgers College admitted that it was limiting the number of Jews in order "to equalize the proportion" and to prevent the university from becoming denominational. In the spring of the following year the college authorities withdrew from this position, which had been vehemently attacked by local and national Jewish agencies. Nonetheless, at the end of a generation of struggle a B'nai B'rith survey in 1946 found that Jews indeed formed about 9% of a U.S. college population that was then slightly over two million, but that they were concentrated (77%) in 50 of the largest schools, and the best smaller schools were still discriminating against them. The proportion of Jews in the professional schools was only 7%, thus indicating that discrimination was still high.

The turning point came that year. Rabbi Stephen S. Wise mounted an attack on Columbia University for practicing unofficial discrimination against Jews by petitioning the city council of the City of New York to withdraw its tax exemption. Columbia had no choice but to announce that the question of religion would no longer figure on any of its application forms. For the flood of soldiers returning from World War II the national government was providing the funds with which to complete their education and the colleges and universities boomed in the next decade. Discrimination against Jews was hard to practice in an era when the educational institutions were seeking the maximum of government funds. In the post-World War II era, faculties were doubling and redoubling, and place was therefore available for Jews. The new postwar industries, especially electronics, required a whole new corps of technicians, and these jobs were staffed without regard to earlier exclusions. By 1968 some opinions were being expressed that the marked presence of Jews everywhere in the professions and the academic world was "arousing some resentment, envy and discontent among less successful non-Jewish faculty members."

It was estimated that by 1972 Jews formed at least 10% of the faculties of all American institutions of higher learning, and that the more highly regarded a school the more nearly likely would it have a Jewish proportion in its faculty reaching 25–50%, the Harvard faculty being probably one third Jewish. Attacks on Jews in academic life and in the professions were mounted largely from within the Negro community, which was demanding place for itself consonant with its proportion in the total population (about 10%), regardless of the results of tests or other screening devices. In this demand Negroes have come into conflict with Jews who have found what contemporary sociologists have called the "meritocracy" useful and convenient. Blacks have succeeded in obtaining a quota of their own, perhaps to some extent at the expense of Jews, in many of the best colleges.

13 DISCRIMINATION

This term refers to distinguishing between people on the basis of the group to which the person belongs rather than individual characteristics. With rare exceptions, contemporary forms of discrimination against Jews were not based upon the type of legal device and sanction that reached its apotheosis with the Nuremberg laws. The postwar disclosure of the details of the Holocaust generated such massive popular revulsion that legal forms of anti-Semitism became taboo, for the gas chambers and the concentration camps were the ultimate consequence of legalized anti-Jewish discrimination. Anti-Semitism continued to find expression in the contemporary world in non-legislative discriminatory patterns. Sophisticated formulations to mask the anti-Semitic intent of the pattern were elaborated, and in no case could the pattern appear to be overtly anti-Semitic. Even where complete or almost complete exclusion of Jews was practiced, the rationale for such action had to be explained on grounds other than religious or ethnic discrimination. The more characteristic pattern took the form of "tokenism" (i.e., the admission of one or a few Jews into a non-Jewish milieu) or a quota system, which restricted the number of Jews to a precise or approximate percentage of the total composition.

The overall pattern of discrimination was selective in character: not all or almost all Jews were the objects of discrimination and not all or almost all spheres of public life were the loci of the discriminatory pattern. There were, however, certain major postwar exceptions to the selective character of non-legislative discrimination. During the "Black Years" in the Soviet Union (1948–53), virtually all

Jews were subject to some form of discrimination, and many were even more harshly treated. A similar phenomenon occurred in Poland during 1968, with the difference that Polish Jews were permitted and even encouraged to emigrate. These anti-Jewish campaigns were deliberately masked, however, in the first case as "anti-Cosmopolitanism," and in the second as "anti-Zionism."

Soviet Union. The Soviet Union, where in 1970 approximately one-quarter of the world's Jewish population lived, offered a classic example of how anti-Semitic motivation on the highest level was expressed in either exclusion, tokenism, or quota techniques. Andrei D. Sakharov, the distinguished Soviet physicist and co-creator of the hydrogen bomb, acknowledged in 1968 that "in the highest bureaucratic elite of [the Soviet] government, the spirit of anti-Semitism was never fully dispelled after the 1930s." A burgeoning Russian nationalism, which fed upon traditional anti-Semitism and was reinforced by the determination to erect barriers against Western influences and contacts, provided the motivation for the policy, as Jews, characteristically, had family as well as spiritual and cultural links with the West. Sakharov specifically mentioned the Soviet Union's "appointments policy" as the device by which discrimination against Jews was effected. That "appointments policy" excluded Jews from all key policy-making positions. Whereas the percentage of Jews in the Central Committee of the Communist Party was 10.8% in 1939, over the course of years, the percentage was reduced to almost nil—only one Jew remained in the Central Committee in 1970. There were no Jews in the Politburo, the Orgburo, or the top levels of the Secretariat. In the sensitive areas of diplomacy, security, foreign trade, and military affairs there were virtually no Jews: at the top levels, there was none at all; elsewhere in the hierarchy there were less than a handful. The political sphere, which embraced soviets on various levels and which was manipulated by the Communist Party apparatus, was characterized by "tokenism," whereby a tiny percentage of Jews was selected by the 171 party. In contrast with the composition of the Supreme Soviet in 1937, for example, when approximately 3.5% of the deputies were Jewish (before the new "appointments policy" had been instituted), at the end of the 1960s, with a membership of some 1,500, it contained a token number of Jews—0.25%. The same percentage obtained in the Supreme Soviets of the 15 Union Republics, in which there were 14 out of some 5,300 deputies; one or two Jewish deputies were chosen for some of the Union Republic Supreme Soviets. On the bottom of the legislative scale, the local soviets, which comprised over 2,000,000 members, received a similar token number of Jews (about 8,000). The percentage on this level approximated that of Jews in the legislatures on the republic and national levels. The quota system was used in the various branches of administration. Yekaterina Furtseva, minister of culture from 1960, explained how the system was initiated. If "a heavy concentration of Jewish people" was found in a governmental department, "steps were taken to transfer them to other enterprises . . . " At about the same time, Canadian Communist Party leader J. B. Salsberg was told in Moscow that the "transfer" method was applied to Jews in the "once-backward" Union Republics in order to make room for the newly trained native cadres in the administrative apparatus. In December 1962, Premier Nikita Khrushchev told Soviet intellectuals that Kremlin policy was aimed at preventing too many Jews from holding prominent posts, and in June 1963, the Party's principal theoretical journal, *Kommunist,* admitted the widespread use of the quota system in the training and placement of cadres in the various Union Republics. The quota system was most clearly expressed in university admission practices. The Soviet *Bulletin of Higher Education* (December 1963) disclosed that "annually planned preferential admission quotas" prevailed in Soviet universities. Nicholas de Witt, a U.S. specialist on Soviet educational practices, explained that the quota system operated "to the particularly severe disadvantage of the Jewish population." In a study published in 1964, he found that "in those republics where Jews constitute an above-average proportion of the urban population, their representation among university students is well below the rate of the general population's access to higher education." Whereas in 1935 the Jewish enrollment in Soviet universities was 13% of the population, by the 1960s it dropped drastically to little more than 3%.

The pattern of discrimination against Jews in political and social life paralleled a policy that deprived the Jewish community of the ethnic and religious rights to which it was constitutionally entitled and that other Soviet ethnic and major religious groups enjoyed. It should be emphasized, however, that the pattern of discrimination, especially in the civic and political arenas, was not endemic to Communist societies. In other European Communist countries (including Poland until 1967–68), Jews held prominent positions at all levels of the party and state administration. Even in the U.S.S.R. the anti-Jewish pattern of discrimination did not extend to everyday channels of social life. Residential restrictions were nonexistent, and there were no barriers to membership and participation in the lower levels of the Communist Party, trade unions, armed forces, social services, and clubs. Employment opportunities, other than administration, in such fields as science, medicine, law, and the arts were widespread. Particularly in the crucial area of the sciences, Jews ranked high both in absolute and relative terms, although the quota system in university admission practices brought about a decline in the percentage of Jews in relation to other nationalities.

United States. This Soviet pattern of discrimination was in striking contrast with the pattern prevailing in the United States, where in 1970 one-half of the world's Jewish population resided. Discrimination against Jews on the national political level was neither existent nor sanctioned. Jews played an important and active role in all areas of political, public, and community life, although to a lesser extent outside major population centers. Yet the chauvinism of an old, established patrician class, combined with a 173 nativist-Populist tradition and an "in-group" phobia of those striving to protect their insecure status (in an extended period of upward social mobility), perpetuated patterns of social discrimination against Jews in non-government spheres—employment, housing, and social institutions. The techniques employed were exclusion, tokenism, and the quota system. Widespread patterns of discrimination in private industry were notable principally on the executive or management levels; no problem was apparent below that level. A study published in 1968 showed that comparatively few Jews were found in executive positions in the insurance, automobile, and shipping industries. A 1967 survey of 38 major companies in the New York City area, including utility and transportation companies, commercial banks, oil concerns, electronic firms, and stock exchanges, revealed that the proportion of Jews among the total number of executives was relatively small. Private employment agencies abetted the perpetuation of discrimination by responding positively to the real or imagined prejudices of their clients. Exclusive residential areas, both in suburbia and high-rental urban cooperatives, were often characterized by quota practices. By means of restrictive covenants, a complete ban on the sale of property to Jews could sometimes be effected. Even though the Supreme Court ruled that covenants were not legally enforceable, the device was still used, as, e.g., in certain choice locations in Washington, D.C. and Detroit. Resort hotels, especially in certain vacation areas, also erected barriers against Jews. A study in 1956–57 showed that one out of four hotels carried on such practices, with an even higher ratio in Arizona resort hotels. Particularly distinctive on the social landscape was the pattern of discrimination in country clubs and city social clubs. According to a 1961 survey, three-quarters of the former and 60% of the latter either excluded Jews or maintained quotas against them. A study released in 1969 emphasized that discrimination in these clubs led to an

174 "almost insurmountable barrier" for Jews who strove for

advancement in industry and finance. The reason for this crucial linkage between social-club discrimination and employment opportunities was the fact that top-level business executives frequented these clubs and "naturally turned to the ranks of those they knew." In local communities, social clubs were vital factors in the power structure, and the scope of Jewish participation in the local decision-making process was directly proportionate to the extent that they excluded or restricted Jews. Progress in removing barriers against Jews, however, was made gradually, especially in the employment field. Other private forms of social discrimination had greatly declined by 1970. Typical of this trend were university admission practices. An American Council on Education study in 1949 revealed that the average Jewish university applicant had considerably less chance of being accepted than a Catholic or Protestant of comparable scholastic ability. The technique generally used was a fixed quota. Since then, and especially from the 1960s, restrictions based upon religion or ethnic origin were significantly reduced. Similarly, anti-Jewish discrimination by fraternities on campuses dropped considerably.

England. The American pattern of social discrimination was paralleled, at least to some extent, in the United Kingdom. In the early 1960s it was estimated that approximately one-half of British golf clubs prevented, as far as possible, the admission of Jews to membership. Usually a quota system was applied, although in Manchester nearly 100 clubs adhered to an unwritten "Aryan paragraph" providing for total exclusion. Whether and to what extent there was a decline in club discrimination from the middle and late 1960s was never studied. Private school (called "public" school in England) enrollment was also characterized by a form of snobbish discrimination effected by the quota system. A London newspaper study in the late 1950s showed that the best-known boys' "public" schools limited the number of Jewish students to 10–15%. Some girls' "public" schools excluded Jews entirely, while others placed a 10 % quota on them. The absence of careful studies 175 on "executive suite" discrimination made judgment about employment practices in England difficult, although in the 1960s relatively few Jews were found in finance and heavy industry. It can be surmised, however, that this problem and related forms of social discrimination were less pressing than in the United States. As in America, the political sphere was virtually devoid of discrimination. The basic motivation of discrimination in England appeared to be social, a vestige of patrician snobbishness perhaps reinforced by religious considerations. The extent to which the American pattern of social discrimination was present in other Western and Latin American countries was not made the object of any scientific study.

Arab Countries. Whereas anti-Semitism in most parts of the Jewish-populated world was expressed by subtler forms of discrimination, in the Arab countries the necessity for pretense was not felt especially after the Six-Day War (1967). Discrimination against Jews was open, callous, and frequently brutal. Upon the establishment of the State of Israel, all the Jews in Iraq were classed as enemy aliens. This act was accompanied by the sequestration of Jewish property and businesses and the banning of emigration. In March 1950, when the ban was lifted for one year, almost all of Iraq's 120,000 Jews fled, leaving 6,000 in the country. Further anti-Jewish discriminatory legislation was enacted in the years that followed, while the outflow of Jews continued, and as of May 1967, the 2,500 remaining Iraqi Jews faced sharp limitations in the areas of citizenship, travel, and property. The Six-Day War brought on even more repressive measures: all Jewish homes were placed under surveillance; telephones were disconnected; personal property could not be sold; assets were frozen; licenses were canceled; the dismissal of Jewish employees was ordered; and travel from their area of residence was forbidden. A complete ban on emigration made the discriminatory pressures under which Jews lived all the more burdensome. Several Jews were publicly hanged in Baghdad, together with Muslim opponents of the regime, as "imperialist and Zionist spies." The situation in Syria was similar. Even prior to the Six-Day War, Syrian Jews were forbidden to sell property and move about beyond a one-and-a-half-mile radius from their place of residence without a special permit. Jews were required to carry special identity cards, and after the war, the 4,000 Syrian Jews were not permitted to emigrate. Just prior to the Six-Day War, the UAR conducted a registration of its 2,500 Jews and, within two or three days of the outbreak of hostilities, ordered the imprisonment of the great majority of Jewish males. Most of these prisoners were released during 1968 but others were kept in prison until 1969 and 1970. Prior to the war, the 4,000-member Jewish community in Libya was subject to a variety of restrictions, including a ban on emigration. The outbreak of war unleashed popular violence against Jews. When the ban on emigration was lifted soon after the war ended, the entire Jewish community fled. The tiny Jewish community of Aden underwent a similar experience.

14 THEORY OF RACE

Nowadays, although there are numerous anthropologists who differ over the exact number and subdivisions of the races of humanity, most are agreed that the characteristics which distinguish races are limited to physical features, color of skin and eye, etc. This conclusion is, however, of comparatively recent date. In the 18th century the "founding fathers" of anthropology almost all believed that the human races differed in innate intelligence, or even in virtue. Obviously the idea of such racial differences is far older than the first attempts at their scientific classification.

Early Beliefs. Primitive tribes who laid claim to particular genealogies, going back to legendary ancestors, developed these ideas in their own way. In classical Greece philosophers like Plato and Aristotle were "racists" in the modern sense of the word: according to Aristotle, the Greeks were born to be free while the Barbarians were slaves by nature. However, in the melting pot of Alexander's empire and later in the Roman empire, belief in ethnocentrism faded; this was especially true of Stoic philosophy. The Jewish tradition, with its majestic story of Adam which furnished all men with a common ancestor, can be considered the first historical example of a fundamentally "anti-racist" conception. On this subject the Talmud states: "for the sake of peace among creatures, the descent of all men is traced back to one individual, so that one may not say to his neighbor, my father is greater than yours" (Sanh. 4:5). Belief in a common descent from Adam was taken over by Christianity and became one of the fundamentals of the Christian principle of the equality of all men before God. However, at the same time, medieval society was divided into three estates—commoners, clergy, and nobility—superiority being ascribed to the "blue blood" of the latter. As most of Europe's reigning monarchs were of Germanic origin, there was a tendency apparent from the earliest days to accord a measure of preeminence to "Germanic blood." Conflicts between such conceptions of degree and the Christian universalist principle were particularly acute in the 16th-century Spanish empire. It was only after lengthy struggles and theological discussions that the Spaniards recognized the native races they found in America as men endowed with souls. At the same time, through statutes dealing with racial purity *(limpieza de sangre)*, a system of racial discrimination was instituted in Spain, applying to the descendants of Jews and Moors who had been converted to Christianity. In spite of their baptism, the blood of these "new Christians" was considered impure and their race inferior.

Eighteenth-Century Anthropological Theories. So, during the whole of European history, it is possible to speak of latent, or even open, racial prejudice. The establishment of the anthropological sciences in the 18th century enabled these prejudices to be expressed systematically, and the systems of classification worked out by the scientists Buffon and Linné were typical in this respect. Both men coupled features (color of skin, type of hair, etc.) with mental and moral characteristics, which were interpreted in favor of the white man of Europe. Buffon, whose system was more overtly racial than Linné's, even considered the white man as the norm, the "king of the creation," and colored men as members of degenerate races. The tendency to regard the white race as superior characterized the majority of anthropological systems elaborated during the 18th and 19th centuries. The rejection of biblical anthropology favored this trend, because then it became possible to attribute different origins to different races. Thus, according to Goethe, Adam was the ancestor of the Jews only, while Voltaire believed that black men were an intermediate species between white men and apes. In the 18th century the 179 major systems of classification (of which the best known and least marred by racial value judgments was that of Blumenbach) distinguished between only four or five principal races. The Jews were usually included in the white race, in whose midst they were supposed to form a nation *sui generis*. But at the beginning of the 19th century, with the emergence of nationalistic struggles, writers began to multiply the number of races, to distinguish between different European races and even to set one against the other. There was continuous interaction in this field between the mental climate of the time, itself closely related to political upheavals, and the current intellectual theories.

Nineteenth-Century Nationalism. From then on racist or quasi-racist notions took root, especially in Germany where nationalist agitators like E. M. Arndt and F. L. Jahn extolled the merits and qualities of the Teutonic race. The philosopher Fichte elaborated a patriotic theory postulating that German was the original language of Europe *(Ursprache)* and the Germans its original people *(Urvolk)*. After 1815, many German students and academics propounded these opinions as part of the Pan-Germanic movement. Ideas of the same type also spread in other countries. After the restoration of the monarchy in France some bourgeois intellectuals, reacting against the pretensions of the "Frankish" nobility, claimed to belong to the native "Gallic" race. In Britain "Germanism" or "Teutonism" found influential supporters in Thomas Carlyle and Thomas Arnold. In some other English circles the "Hebrew race," which had given the West its spiritual values, was championed by Benjamin Disraeli: "All is race, there is no other truth" was his maxim. In that age the concept of "race" was espoused by numerous authors as a substitute for divine providence as the determining factor in history. Germany continued to be the principal nursery of racist theories reinforced by scientific pretensions, partly because its political divisions before 1871 stimulated nationalist fervor, and partly because according to the most prevalent notions the Germans were the only European nation who could claim to be a wholly "pure" race, that is, purely Teutonic. Heinrich Heine commented ironically: "We Germans are the strongest and wisest race; descendants of our princely house sit on all European thrones; our Rothschilds control all the world's stock markets; our scholars lead in all sciences; we know it all."

"Aryan" and "Semite." It is obvious that from then on the Jews were considered as a race apart, an oriental one, and the spectacle of their success in all walks of life after emancipation strengthened the tendency to attribute to them certain specific—and detrimental—racial characteristics. In intellectual spheres the racist theories of the 19th century received a powerful impetus and gained a new orientation from the linguistic discovery of the Indo-European group of languages. A confusion arose between languages and races, a mistake which had grave consequences. It was believed that the nations who spoke European languages, which were thought to have derived from Sanskrit, belonged to the Indo-European or "Aryan" race. In opposition to them was a "Semitic" race, represented by the Jews and the Arabs. Typically enough, German scholars used the term "Indo-Germanic" instead of Indo-European. Of course it was also taken for granted that the "Aryan" race was morally superior to the "Semitic" one. Thus, according to the famous oriental scholar Lassen, "the Semites do not possess that harmonious equilibrium between all the powers of the intellect which characterized the Indo-Germans." His well-known French colleague Ernest Renan spoke of the "appalling simplicity of the Semitic mind." All original creations of the human spirit—with the possible exception of religion—were attributed to the "Aryans." Moreover, many authors considered that, to preserve their special qualities, the Aryan nations must avoid intermingling with the people of an "inferior race." They accorded the Germans the distinction of being the purest Aryans.

Such were the opinions, which, pushed to their limits, were developed and popularized by Comte de Gobineau in his infamous *Essai sur l'Inégalité des Races Humaines* (1853–55). The racial theories of the 19th century tended to establish a double hierarchy: the superiority of the "Aryans" over "Semites" and other "inferior races;" and the superiority of the "Germans" over other "Aryans." The political and economic success (especially after 1871) of the nations who spoke Germanic languages and who therefore considered themselves as belonging to the Teutonic race helped to sanction these opinions. In Latin countries efforts were made to set up a rival hierarchy (which gave rise to the myths of "Latinity" and "Celticity") or, especially in France, to proclaim the superiority of a "racial mixture" over "racial homogeneity." Similarly, in the United States, the adherents of the "melting-pot" conception of the country (limited to the white race) were in conflict with the acolytes of the "Anglo-Saxon race." All these notions continued to be based on the tenacious confusion, typical of the materialist orientation of anthropological science in the 19th century, between "races" and languages or cultures.

However, during the same century, progress in anthropology, ethnography, and prehistory made most specialists gradually abandon these simplified conceptions. Thus the distinguished philologist Max Mueller, although he had previously supported such theories, announced in 1871 that it was absurd to speak of an "Aryan race" or of a "grammar based on the size of the head." However, the "Aryan theory" continued to gain adherents among the general public. It was propagated in every country in school textbooks, which usually summarily repeated ancient opinions and classified Europeans as "Aryans," all except the "Semitic" Jews. The anti-Jewish campaigns, from then on styled "anti-Semitic," made their contribution to the spread of the theory. As a result of all this, by 1900 the existence of an "Aryan race" was firmly established in the public mind as a scientific truth. Usually, this only implied a vague belief in the intellectual or moral superiority of the "Aryans" over the "Semites," and a more marked superiority of the "Whites" over the "Yellows" and especially the "Blacks." But in the arena of the violent anti-Semitic campaigns of the time, some fanatics worked out elaborate eschatological systems in which the struggle between the Aryan and Semitic races was the counterpart of the final struggle between Good and Evil. The most influential of these writers was the Anglo-German Houston Stewart Chamberlain, who stated that the original sin of the Jews was that from ancient times they had been a mixed race opposed to Aryan purity. Ingenuously, in the time of King Cyrus, the Aryans had committed the fatal blunder of protecting the Jews: "... under the protection of Aryan tolerance was planted the seed from which Semitic intolerance spread its poison over the earth for thousands of years, a curse on all that was noble and a shame to Christianity."

From the second quarter of the 20th century scientific anthropology rid itself almost entirely of the dangerous error of dividing the human races into "superior" and "inferior," or even "good" and "bad." At that same time, however, in a defeated and disoriented Germany, gripped by unemployment, this same error helped to weld a political party and then grew into a state dogma. Thus, from 1933 the theory of race was nothing but a kind of totemistic mythology, serving to justify an imperialistic and murderous expansionism.

However, the racial tensions occasioned in the United States by the struggle of blacks for increased rights did again raise the issue of race, on theoretical grounds, in the 1960s. At least two serious scholars, Carleton S. Coon and Arthur R. Jensen, argued on the basis of statistical evidence that the physical and mental characteristics of blacks differed from those of whites and that the capacity of blacks to absorb education was different from that of whites. Against such notions other scholars argued that the tests used to determine intellectual capacity were themselves biased in favor of western, bourgeois, cultural norms. The presumption that there is any important reality to racial differences continued to be denied by the bulk of American scholarship, largely on the moral ground that to take such differences seriously and to presume that change in environment and increased educational opportunity could not ultimately give individuals of all the races equality of personal opportunity was an offense to democracy. Nonetheless the discussion of racial difference, which was completely taboo in the U.S. in the generation which had witnessed Hitler and which looked to a peaceful and gradualist solution of the "Negro problem," is now again a matter of debate.

15 NEO-FASCISM

In the postwar world all radical right-wing movements, irrespective of their doctrinal contents and differences—except those explicitly aiming at the restoration of an anti-Semitic, racialist, Nazi-type dictatorship (see Neo-Nazism) are commonly referred to as "neo-Fascist." They share an attitude of extreme, militant nationalism; a belief in authoritarian rather than democratic government; and a total rejection of socialist, particularly Marxist, dogma with its underlying universalist and egalitarian ethos. Inhabiting the social periphery between the middle and the working class, Neo-Fascism appeals mostly to those deprived of their former independent status (as artisans, white-collar workers, small-holders, craftsmen, etc.) by the growth of an urban, industrialized society and driven to xenophobia and hostility toward minority groups, which they believe to have either caused their social and economic decline or contributed to it. Hatreds vary according to demographic conditions. In the United States and Britain, Neo-Fascist movements have a strong anti-color bias, whereas similar French groups in the 1950s and early 1960s were anti-Algerian and in Switzerland these prejudices inspired agitation against alien workers. Anti-Semitism is almost always implicit in such attitudes and it can easily become, as in the case of the Argentinian Tacuara or the Swedish Nordiska Rikspartiet (Nordic Realm Party), an ideological focal point. In the West, the shock of the Nazi Holocaust militated after World War II against the spread of Neo-Fascist movements, particularly obsessively anti-Semitic ones; however, the Israel-Arab Six-Day War (1967) modified this trend. Formerly disreputable anti-Semitic prejudices relabeled "anti-Zionism" became respectable again when disseminated by the Communist establishment, the New Left, and Black Power activists. Arab anti-Israel propaganda agencies, until 1967 associated with the extreme right, have since—and without breaking their Neo-Fascist links—been courted and supported by the radical left as well.

Neo-Fascism survived best in Italy. The Movimento Sociale Italiano (MSI) obtained close to 1,500,000 votes (5.2% of the total poll) in the 1970 provincial elections, sending 32 deputies to the regional councils. However, neither occasional swastika-daubing forays into Rome's old ghetto (1958, 1960) nor parliamentary representation dating back to the early 1950s elevated the MSI to a significant position. Further to the right, the minuscule Ordine Nuovo (New Order), formed by activist dissidents from the MSI, is a terrorist, but otherwise negligible, force, cultivating links with like-minded European "New Order" movements. Prince Valerio Borghese, a former honorary MSI president, founded the militant National Front which made an abortive attempt to overthrow the government (December, 1970). In France the horrors of Nazi occupation inhibited the revival of overtly Fascist movements. Efforts by the Sidos brothers to channel resentments over the loss of empire (Indochina, North Africa) into the Neo-Fascist Jeune Nation failed, while the less clearly defined anti-establishment campaign of Pierre Poujade won 60 parliamentary seats (1956). Both his party and the anti-Gaullist extremists of the Algérie-Française OAS had Fascist and anti-Semitic overtones, but neither survived the nationalist appeal of de Gaulle's presidency. In the post-de Gaulle era, Ordre Nouveau, the successor organization to the Occident (banned 1968), gained some notoriety for militancy and street-fighting.

Neo-Fascism also failed to prosper in postwar England. Sir Oswald Mosley's once powerful British Union of Fascists, renamed British Union, had dwindled into irrelevance. A number of extremist organizations like the

Empire Loyalists, the British National Party, and the Racial Preservation Society (whose street-fighting propensities gained them brief notoriety in the early 1960s), combined in 1967 to form the National Front, without, however, making any impact on national politics. In the 1970 general election the Front put up ten candidates, none of whom polled more than 1,600 votes. In the United States, the extremist right exists both inside and outside the two traditional (Republican, Democratic) parties, and is preoccupied mainly with the Negro problem and the black-white confrontation. It considers the white liberals and militant Negroes as its main enemy. Old-style primitive anti-Semitism, however, still flourishes among such movements as the Ku Klux Klan and the Christian Crusader, but the more sophisticated John Birch Society vent their anti-Jewish resentments on the "liberal establishment" represented as predominantly Jewish. The Klans, Crusaders, and Birchists are typically U.S. phenomena; lacking any party organization able to attain power, they cannot be regarded as true neo-Fascists.

16 NEO-NAZISM

This is a new Nazi movement that has emerged after World War II and is based on anti-Semitic doctrines similar to those propounded in Hitler's *Mein Kampf* and exemplified in the structure and aspirations of the Third Reich. Since Neo-Nazism's appeal, like that of Nazism, is specifically German, it is in Germany that one would expect the movement to flourish. However, as incitement to race hatred, as well as any attempt to resuscitate the Nazi Party, are explicitly outlawed by the Constitution and the criminal laws of the German Federal Republic (as well as in the Communist German Democratic Republic), no party overtly attempting to revive Nazism can legally exist there. Although National Socialist parties openly propagating anti-Semitism, displaying the swastika flags, and glorifying Nazi achievements sprang up under Colin Jordan in Great Britain and Lincoln Rockwell (murdered in 1967) in the United States, both have been utterly inconsequential fringe movements, of interest to the social pathologist rather than the student of politics.

Allowing for a broader definition, Neo-Nazism has come to be identified with German anti-Semitic ultranationalist, extreme right-wing movements, whether made up of old or new Nazis. Without seriously threatening the still fragile German democracy, a number of such movements gained some short-lived popularity and notoriety. The first to draw, if somewhat unwittingly, ex-Nazis into a political party was Alfred Loritz, a confused demagogue with an anti-Nazi record. His Bavarian *Economic Reconstruction Association,* founded in 1945 with U.S. consent, denounced Allied policies and articulated the widespread economic discontent of the "pre-economic-miracle" era. The "blonde Hitler," as he was sometimes called, frightened the young republic and the world at large when he gained 14.4% of the vote in his native Bavaria, winning 12 seats in the Bundestag, after the first German general election (1949). The lack of positive policies, however, coupled with internal dissensions, rent the party asunder long before it failed to gain a single seat in the following (1953) general election.

Similarly spectacular and ominous was Fritz Dorls' deliberate attempt to revive Nazism through the Socialist Reich Party (SRP). Its leadership was made up entirely of old Nazis, the most prominent of whom was the deputy chairman, Ernst Rhemer, the Wehrmacht officer who successfully thwarted the July 20, 1944, plot against Hitler. Apart from distributing anti-Semitic election leaflets, reminiscent of *Der Stürmer,* the SRP even boasted a gang organized on storm-troop lines, the so-called Reichsfront. In 1951 when the SRP gained 11% of the Lower Saxony vote, an alarmed federal government contested the party's legality before the Constitutional Court. Declared illegal as an attempt to reestablish the proscribed Nazi Party, this particular specter of resurgent Nazism disappeared. It reappeared a year later when the British arrested Dr. Naumann, one of Dr. Goebbels' top-ranking officials, whose plot to subvert the respectable Free Democratic Party by infiltrating ex-Nazis into key positions was well on the way to succeeding.

In the 1960s the spectacular and unexpected success of the NDP (National Democratic Party of Germany) aroused worldwide fears of a Nazi revival. Founded in 1965 by Adolf von Thadden to unite the hitherto splintered and ineffectual "nationalist opposition," the party shocked the German and world opinion when in the 1966–67 *Land* elections it gained admission to a number of *Land* parliaments by substantially exceeding the required 5% of the vote. Careful not to fall foul of the Constitutional Court, the NPD, run largely by ex-Nazis, appealed to exactly the same prejudices and self-assertions to which Germans responded so overwhelm- 189 ingly in the Hitler era. Jews were not openly denigrated, but the State of Israel and its policies were viciously attacked. The "domination by alien big powers," reminiscent of the Nazi fiction of "Judean-Marxist world conspiracy," was denounced, as were references to Nazi crime. The party manifesto demanded "an end to the lie of Germany's exclusive guilt which serves to extort continuously thousands of millions from our people," apparently a reference to restitution and compensation payment to Israel and individual Jews. Beset like its predecessors by internecine leadership struggles and lacking forward-looking policies, the NPD failed to gain the qualifying 5% in the 1969 general election. This failure led to a crisis of confidence, which resulted in the party losing its seats in the various *Land* parliaments after the 1970 elections. At that time it was doubtful whether Neo-Nazism still commanded a politically meaningful potential, although the phenomenon still lingered on in violently "anti-Israel" weeklies (like the *Deutsche National Zeitung*) or in the publications of ex-Reich press chief Suedermann's Druffel Verlag and similar publishing houses.

In Austria, Neo-Nazism lacked the organizational framework or a sufficiently numerous following to qualify as a politically relevant force. Among the minuscule groupings more or less openly committed to propagating Nazi ideas and extolling Nazi achievements, Theodor Soucek's Sozialorganische Bewegung Europas (SOBRE) was perhaps the most noteworthy in the early 1950s. It tried to coordinate efforts of Nazi collaborators and sympathizers in the former occupied territories to revitalize the Hitlerian "new order" in the context of the then emerging Europe. SOBRE enjoyed the support of Konrad Windisch, one of the founders of the Bund Heimattreuer Jugend (BHJ), whose initials HJ (for Hitler Jugend) proclaimed its ideological lineage and identification. Despite the insignificance of these movements, residual anti-Semitism and subliminal Nazi sympathies seemed to be more widespread in Austria than 190 in Germany, thus the marked reluctance of Austrian authorities to prosecute and of juries to convict such war criminals and Eichmann aides as Murer, Novak, or Raiakovic and the parsimoniousness of Austrian restitution.

Argentina figured prominently in the Nazis' plans to save the movement and themselves after defeat. This tied in well with President Peron's dreams of Argentinian hegemony based on a modernized army and an independent armament industry, which the Nazi experts were to develop. Nazis headed nuclear research institutes, while World War II air aces like Rudel and Galland advised the Argentinian air force and Professor Tank, a German jet designer, started an Argentinian aircraft industry. Eichmann and his aides (Klingenfuss, Rademacher, and Dr. Mengele) found sanctuary, while Johannes von Leers, head of an anti-Jewish department in Goebbel's Propaganda Ministry, became Peron's adviser. Moreover, the Nazi gospel continued to be preached in German in *Der Weg* (Buenos Aires) and other Duerer Verlag publications. After Peron's fall (1955), some of these fugitives moved to Egypt (a Nazi sanctuary since 1945), where military needs and anti-Israel, anti-Semitic resentments offered them scope. Years later the effort of ex-Nazis to develop Egyptian jet engines, supersonic fighters, and rockets (the Messerschmidt, Brandner, and Pilz teams) caused greater international consternation than the activities of von Leers and S. S. General Bender in the Egyptian Ministry of National Guidance or of the former Gestapo chief Sellman as a police adviser on "anti-Jewish action." On the whole, however, by the early 1970s Neo-Nazism seemed to be declining.

Appendix A: The Dreyfus Affair

During the summer of 1894 a secret military document (known as the *bordereau*) sent by a French officer to the military attaché of the German embassy in Paris, Col. von Schwartzkoppen, fell into the hands of the French Intelligence Service. On the basis of a certain similarity of handwriting, and probably out of anti-Jewish prejudice against Dreyfus, the heads of the Intelligence Service—among whom Major H. J. Henry was conspicuous—threw suspicion upon Dreyfus. Alfred Dreyfus was the son of a wealthy, assimilated Alsatian family. He had entered the army in 1892 and became a captain on the general staff, where he was the only Jew. He was arrested and tried before a court-martial.

Dreyfus' trial took place in Paris *in camera* and the testimonies were insufficiently verified. It was also not disclosed that contrary to all legal procedure the ministry of war had placed a file of secret documents (part of which were forgeries) before the tribunal, a fact concealed even from Dreyfus' attorney. The court unanimously found Dreyfus guilty of treason, and he was sentenced to life imprisonment. On January 5, 1895, Dreyfus was publicly demoted in a degrading ceremony, during which he continued to proclaim, "I am innocent." The mob, which had been incited by the anti-Semitic press, especially by E. A. Drumont, accompanied the ceremony with fulminations against Dreyfus and the Jews. Dreyfus was exiled to Devil's Island (French Guinea, off the coast of South America), even though in the meanwhile, the German ambassador had declared formally that Germany had had no contact with Dreyfus.

Dreyfus' brother turned to the writer Bernard Lazare, who now led the struggle against the verdict. In November 1896 Lazare published a pamphlet, "The Truth about the Dreyfus Affair," and sent it to members of the senate and public figures. The new head of the French Intelligence Service, Lt. Col. Georges Picquart, had independently sensed something suspicious in the Dreyfus trial. In March

1896, Intelligence Service personnel seized a letter which Schwartzkoppen had written to a French major, Ferdinand Walsin Esterhazy, an adventurer of aristocratic Hungarian origin. This made it clear that Esterhazy was a German agent. Picquart concluded that the *bordereau* incriminating Dreyfus had been written by Esterhazy. Henry forged additional documents to prove to his superiors that the court-martial had not erred. Picquart was dismissed from his position and dispatched to serve in Africa.

Before leaving Paris he transmitted the facts to his friends. Through them they reached the ears of the left-wing senator, Auguste Scheurer-Kestner, who announced in the senate that Dreyfus was innocent, and openly accused Esterhazy. The right-wing prime minister, F. J. Méline, refused to accept his statement and tried to hide the facts. The Dreyfus case increasingly became the focus of the political struggle centering round the regime, its image and principles, and fought in all strata of French society, including circles close to the government. Esterhazy was tried and acquitted, while Picquart was punished with 60 days imprisonment. On January 13, 1898 *L'Aurore,* Georges Clemenceau's newspaper, published an open letter from the novelist Emile Zola to the president of the republic, captioned *"J'accuse!",* which accused the denouncers of Dreyfus of malicious libel. The article made a powerful impression; 200,000 copies were sold in Paris. Zola was found guilty of libel in February 1898. Officers of the general staff threatened to resign if Dreyfus was acquitted and anti-Semitic riots occurred in different parts of the country. In the meantime confidence in the justice of the verdict was waning. The affair aroused lively interest abroad and in France it became a public issue. Parties, social circles, and even families were split. The antagonistic groups formed two camps—the *Ligue des Droits de l'Homme,* which spearheaded the fight for Dreyfus, and the *Ligue de la Patrie Française,* led by Paul Déroulède. Many of the supporters of the latter camp considered that a single case of injustice involving one Jew was not sufficient grounds 193

Emile Zola's open letter *J'Accuse!* published on the front page
of the Paris newspaper *L'Aurore*, Jan. 13, 1898. The letter pas-
sionately proclaimed Dreyfus' innocence and accused his denouncers of malicious libel. Jerusalem, J.N.U.L.

for staining the honor of the army.

In summer 1898 the protestations of Picquart and others
induced the new war minister, Cavaignac, to reopen the
case and re-investigate the documents. Henry's forgeries
were detected. He was arrested and subsequently committed suicide in his cell. Public opinion moved in Dreyfus'
favor and the controversy divided the government. At last
the government decided to request an annulment of the
verdict and a retrial for Dreyfus from the Supreme Court.
The political agitation continued, and after several crises
René Waldeck-Rousseau formed a cabinet whose avowed
aim was to restore the rule of law and justice and
reestablish democracy.

THE SECOND TRIAL. The second trial took place in
Rennes. The army officers adhered to their original testimony. Finally, on September 9, 1899, the court-martial decided

Lithograph of Dreyfus' second trial before a court-martial at Rennes, 1899. On the left, Major Carrière, public prosecutor, addresses the court; behind Dreyfus are Edgar Demange and Ferdinand Labori, defense counsel. New York, Leo Baeck Institute.

by a majority that Dreyfus had committed treason—but because of "extenuating circumstances" he was sentenced to only ten years' imprisonment, five of which he had already served. Anti-Semites and reactionaries viewed the verdict as a justification of their position. Differences of opinion developed between Dreyfus' defenders: those to whom the Dreyfus affair was a political issue and a matter of principle wanted him to appeal and continue the struggle, while Dreyfus and his family were interested only in securing his release. At Waldeck-Rousseau's suggestion, Dreyfus withdrew his appeal and was finally granted a "pardon" by the president of the republic. In 1904, with the

Leftist government firmly established, Dreyfus demanded a fresh investigation. The Court of Appeal reexamined the case, and in 1906 pronounced that the evidence against Dreyfus was completely unsubstantiated and that it was unnecessary to order a further trial to exonerate him.

The Dreyfus affair was a turning point in the history of the Third Republic. It embittered the struggle between the opponents and partisans of the republican regime. The Waldeck-Rousseau cabinet succeeded in enacting a number of anti-clerical measures, and in 1905 it passed a law separating the church from the state. This also influenced the status of the Jewish Consistory in France. The Dreyfus affair made a powerful impact on the attitude of the socialist parties toward the Jews. The radical Marxist wing under Jules Guèsde, which identified Jews with the capitalists and viewed the affair as an internal concern of the bourgeoisie, retreated before the socialist-humanitarian wing led by Jean-Léon Jaurès. Proletarian anti-Semitism weakened. The Dreyfus affair made a strong impact on the outlook of world Jewry and the atmosphere in their respective countries. Jews everywhere were shocked that the affair could take place in France, the "homeland of liberty and the Great Revolution," and that hatred of the Jews could still prejudice the behavior of a considerable part of the French people, in particular when the Jewish victim was completely assimilated. This seemed to prove clearly that assimilation was no defense against anti-Semitism. Theodor Herzl's confidence in liberalism was shaken when he personally observed the French mass reaction and the uproar that the Dreyfus case aroused. The experience led him to Zionism.

Echoes of the Dreyfus affair continued to reverberate in France for over a generation. Its consequences were still recognizable in the line that divided the Vichy government from the Free French during World War II.

Appendix B: The Beilis Trial

A notorious ritual murder trial. On March 20, 1911, the mutilated body of Andrei Yushchinsky, a 12-year-old boy, was discovered in a cave on the outskirts of Kiev. The monarchist rightist press immediately launched a vicious anti-Jewish campaign, accusing the Jews of using human blood for ritual purposes. At the funeral of Yushchinsky, leaflets circulating the blood libel were distributed by members of the reactionary "Black Hundred" ("Union of Russian People") organization. Meanwhile the police investigation traced the murder to a gang of thieves associated with a woman, Vera Cheberiak, notorious for criminal dealings. However, the reactionary anti-Semitic organizations led by the "Black Hundred" pressured the anti-Semitic minister of justice, I. G. Shcheglovitov, to channel the investigation as a ritual murder charge. Accordingly, the chief district attorney of Kiev disregarded the police information and instead looked for a Jew on whom to shift the crime, through whom the entire Jewish people could be publicly indicted.

In July 1911, a lamplighter testified that on March 12, the day Yushchinsky disappeared, he had seen him playing with two other boys on the premises of the brick kiln owned by a Jew, Zaitsev. He also alleged that a Jew had suddenly appeared and kidnapped Yushchinsky, pulling him toward the brick kiln. On the strength of this testimony, Mendel Beilis, the superintendent of the brick kiln, was arrested on July 21, 1911, and sent to prison, where he remained for over two years. A report was submitted to Czar Nicholas II that Beilis was regarded by the judiciary as the murderer of Yushchinsky.

The case attracted universal attention. Protests and addresses by scientists, public and political leaders, artists, men of letters, clergymen, and other liberal-minded men were published in all the civilized countries of Europe and the United States affirming that the blood libel was baseless. The trial of Beilis took place in Kiev from Sept. 25 through Oct. 28, 1913. The chief prosecutor A. I. Vipper made

197

anti-Jewish statements in his closing address and defended the Cheberiak gang against the charge of Yushchinsky's murder. Beilis was represented by the most able counsels of the Moscow, St. Petersburg, and Kiev bars: Vassily Maklakov, Oscar O. Grusenberg, N. P. Karabchevsky, A. S. Zarundy, and D. N. Grigorovitch-Barsky. The lamplighter and his wife, on whose testimony the indictment of Beilis rested, when questioned by the presiding judge, answered, "We know nothing at all." They confessed that both had been confused by the secret police and made to answer questions they did not comprehend. "Scientific" foundation for the blood libel was supplied at the trial by a Catholic priest with a criminal record, Justin Pranaitis, who stated that the murder of Yushchinsky had all the characteristics of ritual murder enjoined by the Jewish religion. His arguments were refuted by the rabbi of Moscow, Jacob Mazeh, who proved that Pranaitis was ignorant of the talmudic texts cited. Two Russian professors of high standing, Troitsky and Kokovtzoff, also spoke on behalf of the defense in praise of Jewish values and exposed the falsity of the ritual murder hypothesis. The jury, composed of simple Russian peasants, after several hours of deliberation unanimously declared Beilis "not guilty."

Beilis, who still remained in danger of revenge by the "Black Hundred," left Russia with his family for Erez Israel. In 1920 he settled in the United States. Bernard Malamud's novel *The Fixer* is based on the Beilis case.

Appendix C: The Slánský Trial

This trial was the first of a series of anti-Semitic show trials held in Czechoslovakia in the early 1950s whose chief defendant was Rudolf Slánský (1901–1952), secretary-general of the Czechoslovak Communist Party after World War II. Of the 14 leading party members prosecuted for conspiracy against the state, 11 were Jews. Eight of these defendants—Ludvík Frejka, head of the economic department of the President's Office; Bedřich Geminder, head of the party's international department; Bedřich Reicin, deputy defense minister; Rudolf Margolius, deputy minister of foreign trade; Otto Fischl, deputy finance minister; Otto Sling, first secretary of the party in Brno; and André Katz-Simone, a leading Communist journalist, in addition to Slánský himself—were executed. The remaining three Jewish defendants—deputy foreign ministers Arthur London and Vavro Hajdu and deputy minister of foreign trade Evžen Loebl—were sentenced to life imprisonment. Show trials aimed at eradicating the Titoist "heresy" from the leadership of the Soviet satellites were held shortly before in other East European countries (e.g., the Kostov trial in Bulgaria and the Rajk trial in Hungary), but the Slánský trial evolved a distinct anti-Jewish character. Foreign Minister Vlado Clementis, one of the three non-Jewish defendants sentenced to death (the other two being Slánský's deputy, Josef Frank, and deputy security minister Karel Sváb) was accused of Slovak "bourgeois nationalism" and Titoism, and an attempt was made to present him as "the Czechoslovak Rajk." But the main orientation of the prosecution was "anti-Zionist," anti-Israel, and openly anti-Semitic. The Slánský Trial thus formed a direct link with the Doctors' plot and the wave of anti-Semitism which spread throughout the Soviet Union in the last four or five years of Stalin's regime. In these trials, for the first time in the history of Communism, the anti-Semitic accusation of a worldwide Jewish conspiracy was openly proclaimed by an authoritative Communist forum (it was linked by the prosecution with the activities of the

American Jewish Joint Distribution Committee). The Jewish origin of the accused was repeatedly stressed, and their alleged crimes were traced to this prime cause. The prosecution stigmatized the accused as Zionists, although they had never had any connection with the Zionist movement and had, in fact, opposed Zionism all their lives.

The trials were part of an effort to consolidate power inside the Czechoslovak Communist Party in the hands of a group of leaders approved and manipulated from Moscow. The fact that Jews held many key posts in the party and state machinery—although Slánský was the only Jew in the Politbureau at the time—prompted an increase of latent popular anti-Semitism. This circumstance was utilized to strengthen the position of the inner circle of the Communist leadership and to put the blame for the rapidly worsening economic situation on prominent Jewish Communists. The trials were conducted under the direction and supervision of secret agents from Moscow and were also intended to help explain the change of Communist policy toward the State of Israel. The Israel legation in Prague was depicted as a center of espionage and anti-Czechoslovak subversion. Accusations were directed mainly against the first Israel minister in Prague, Ehud Avriel, and his successor, Aryeh Kubovy, who was declared *persona non grata*. Two Israel citizens, Mordekhai Oren and Shimon Orenstein, were arrested, used as prosecution witnesses to prove Slánský's alleged contacts with "Zionist conspirators," and were later sentenced in a separate trial to long prison terms. The trials were a signal for a wave of anti-Jewish persecution. Hundreds of Czechoslovak Jews were thrown into prison or sent, often without trial, to forced labor camps. The situation gradually became less frenzied after Stalin's death; but only at the end of the 1950s, and in some cases even later, were victims of the Slánský Trial rehabilitated. The accusations against the Zionist movement and Israel, however, were not revoked, and relations between Czechoslovakia and Israel remained tense and unfriendly.

Appendix D: The "Doctors' Plot"

One of the most dramatic anti-Jewish episodes in the Soviet Union in the last years of Stalin's regime involving the "unmasking" of a group of prominent Moscow doctors, mostly Jews, as conspiratorial assassins of Soviet leaders. On January 13, 1953, *Pravda* and Radio Moscow announced that nine eminent doctors were under arrest and had confessed to murdering two Soviet leaders of the past, A. S. Shcherbakov and A. A. Zhdanov (who had died in 1945 and 1948, respectively). They were reported to have also admitted conspiring to murder a number of prominent figures in the Soviet armed forces, including the war minister, Marshal A. M. Vasilevski, the chief of staff, General S. M. Shtemenko, and the popular war hero, Marshal I. S. Konev. Six of the nine doctors were Jews. "Most of the participants in the terrorist group," read the statement, "were connected with the international Jewish bourgeois nationalist organization, the 'Joint' (American Jewish Joint Distribution Committee) established by American Intelligence . . . (in order to) conduct extensive espionage terrorist, and other subversive work in many countries including the Soviet Union."

These accusations unleashed panic among the Jews of the Soviet Union and were met by reactions of disbelief and foreboding in Western Europe, the U.S.A., and Israel. On January 19, the Israel foreign minister, Moshe Sharett, bitterly condemned the Soviet action. A bomb exploded in the courtyard of the Soviet embassy in Tel Aviv on February 9, wounding four of the staff. Despite prompt apologies from the Israel government, the U.S.S.R. immediately broke off diplomatic relations. The Soviet press now stepped up its attacks on Israel, the "Joint," Wall Street, Zionism, and imperialism. "The pack of mad dogs from Tel Aviv," wrote Yuri Zhukov in *Pravda,* Feb. 14, 1953, "is loathsome and vile in its thirst for blood." An article published in *Trud* on February 13 noted that the "Joint" had organized major anti-government conspiracies not only in the U.S.S.R. but in Hungary and Czechoslovakia as well 201

— direct reference being made to the Slánský trial of November 1952.

Stalin died on March 5, and on April 3 *Pravda* announced that the doctors were not guilty and had been freed, and those responsible for using "impermissible means of investigation" had been arrested. On July 20 diplomatic relations between Israel and the Soviet Union were restored.

The Plot was apparently part of Stalin's plan for a new purge of the top Soviet leadership. It was probably directed against Lavrentii Beria, the minister of the interior (MVD), who had been responsible for security matters when Shcherbakov and Zhdanov had died. The *Pravda* editorial of January 13 specifically criticized "the agencies of state security" that had failed to "discover the doctors' wrecking, terrorist organization in time." (Moreover, the Plot was clearly modeled on the 1938 case of G. G. Yagoda, an earlier chief of the Secret Police who had been found guilty of recruiting medical specialists to murder such prominent citizens as Maxim Gorki.) Stalin's death enabled Beria to regain control of the Secret Police (MGB) and merge it with his ministry, the MVD. The release of the doctors and the arrest of their interrogators evidently formed part of Beria's desperate, but ultimately futile, effort to consolidate his power. Seen in broader perspective, the Plot proved to be the last of those macabre "conspiracies" that were manufactured during Stalin's reign but did not reappear in such a form in the subsequent Soviet regimes, though many of the anti-Jewish manifestations that had accompanied the Doctor's Plot were to reemerge later.

In his secret speech at the Twentieth Party Congress (1956) Nikita Khrushchev blamed the Doctors' Plot on Stalin, but carefully ignored its anti-Semitic aspects and even took the opportunity to exonerate S. D. Ignatev, who had headed the MGB during the Plot, in early 1953. In fact, Ignatev was reelected to the Party's Central Committee in 1956.

CHRONOLOGY

203

	policy of forcible conversion of all Jews in the kingdom.
624–628	Jewish tribes of Hejaz (Arabia) destroyed by Muhammad.
628	Dagobert I expels Jews from Frankish kingdom.
632	Heraclius, Byzantine emperor, decrees forced baptism of all Jews in the Byzantine empire.
633	Official Church doctrine on conversion of Jews in Spain formulated.
638	Visigothic king Chintila compels the sixth council of Toledo to adopt resolution proclaiming that only Catholics may reside in the kingdom of Spain.
694–711	All Jews under Visigothic rule in Spain declared slaves, their possessions confiscated and the Jewish religion outlawed.
717–20	Caliph Omar II introduces series of discriminatory regulations against the *dhimmi,* the protected Christians and Jews, among them the wearing of a special garb.
1009–13	Fatimid caliph Al-Ḥākim in Erez Israel issues severe restrictions against Jews.
1012	Emperor Henry II of Germany expels Jews from Mainz, the beginning of persecutions against Jews in Germany.
1096–99	First Crusade. Crusaders massacre the Jews of the Rhineland (1096).
1144	Blood libel at Norwich (England); first recorded blood libel.
1146	Anti-Jewish riots in Rhineland by the Crusaders of the second Crusade.
1147	Beginning of the brutal persecutions of the Jews of North Africa under the Almohads, which lasted until 1212.
1182	King Philip Augustus of France decrees the expulsion of the Jews from his kingdom and the confiscation of their real estate.
1190	Anti-Jewish riots in England; massacre at York,

	and other cities.
1215	Fourth Lateran Council introduces the Jewish Badge.
1235	Blood libel at Fulda, Germany.
1236	Severe anti-Jewish persecutions in western France.
1240	Disputation of Paris which led to the burning of the Talmud.
1242	Burning of the Talmud at Paris.
1255	Blood libel at Lincoln, England.
1263	Disputation of Barcelona.
1290	Expulsion of the Jews from England, the first of the great general expulsions of the Middle Ages.
1298–99	Massacre of thousands of Jews in 146 localities in southern and central Germany led by the German knight Rindfleisch.
1306	Expulsion of Jews from France.
1320	Pastoureaux ("Shepherds"), participants of the second Crusade in France against the Muslims in Spain, attack the Jews of 120 localities in southwest France.
1321	Persecutions against Jews in central France in consequence of a false charge of their supposed collusion with the lepers.
1322	Expulsion from the kingdom of France.
1336–39	Persecutions against Jews in Franconia and Alsace led by lawless German bands, the Armleder.
1348–50	Black Death Massacres which spread throughout Spain, France, Germany and Austria, as a result of accusations that the Jews had caused the death of Christians by poisoning the wells and other water sources.
1389	Massacre of the Prague (Bohemia) community.
1391	Wave of massacres and conversions in Spain and Balearic Islands.
1394	Expulsion from the kingdom of France.
1399	Blood libel in Poznan.
1411–12	Oppressive legislation against Jews in Spain as an

	outcome of the preaching of the Dominican friar Vicente Ferrer.
1413–14	Disputation of Tortosa (Spain). The most important and longest of the Christian-Jewish disputations, the consequence of which was mass conversions and intensified persecutions.
1421	Persecutions of Jews in Vienna and its environs, confiscation of their possessions, and forcible conversion of Jewish children, 270 Jews burnt at stake, known as the *Wiener Gesera* (Vienna edict). Expulsion of Jews from Austria.
1435	Massacre and conversion of the Jews of Majorca.
1438	Establishment of mellahs (ghettos) in Morocco.
1452–53	John of Capistrano, Italian Franciscan friar, incites persecutions and expulsions of Jews from cities in Germany.
1473	Marranos of Valladolid and Cordoba, in Spain, massacred.
1474	Marranos of Segovia, Spain, massacred.
1480	Inquisition established in Spain.
1483	Torquemada appointed inquisitor general of Spanish Inquisition. Expulsion of Jews from Warsaw.
1490–91	Blood libel in La Guardia, town in Spain, where the alleged victim became revered as a saint.
1492	Expulsion from Spain.
1492–93	Expulsion from Sicily.
1495	Expulsion from Lithuania.
1496–97	Expulsion from Portugal; mass forced conversion.
1506	Massacre of Marranos in Lisbon.
1510	Expulsion of Jews from Brandenburg (Germany).
1516	Venice initiates the ghetto, the first in Christian Europe.
1531	Inquisition established in Portugal.
1535	Jews of Tunisia expelled and massacred.
1541	Expulsion from the kingdom of Naples. Expulsion from Prague and crown cities.
1544	Martin Luther, German religious reformer, attacks

	the Jews with extreme virulence.
1550	Expulsion from Genoa (Italy).
1551	Expulsion from Bavaria.
1553	Burning of the Talmud in Rome.
1554	Censorship of Hebrew books introduced in Italy.
1556	Burning of Marranos at Ancona, Italy.
1567	Expulsion from the republic of Genoa (Italy).
1569 and 1593	Expulsion from the Papal States (Italy).
1614	Vincent Fettmilch, anti-Jewish guild leader in Frankfort, Germany, attacks with his followers the Jews of the Town and forces them to leave the city.
1624	Ghetto established at Ferrara (Italy).
1648–49	Massacres initiated by Bogdan Chmielnicki, leader of the Cossacks, and peasant uprising against Polish rule in the Ukraine, in which 100,000 Jews were killed and 300 communities destroyed.
1650	Jews of Tunisia confined to special quarters *(Ḥāra)*
1655 56	Massacres of Jews during the wars of Poland against Sweden and Russia.
1670	Expulsion from Vienna; Blood libel at Metz (France).
1711	Johann Andreas Eisenmenger writes his *Entdecktes Judenthum* ("Judaism Unmasked"), a work denouncing Judaism and which had a formative influence on modern anti-Semitic polemics.
1712	Blood libel in Sandomierz (Poland) after which the Jews of the town were expelled.
1715	Pope Pius VI issues a severe "Edict concerning the Jews," in which he renews all former restrictions against them.
1734–36	Haidamacks, paramilitary bands in Polish Ukraine, attack Jews.
1745	Expulsion from Prague.
1768	Haidamacks massacre the Jews of Uman (Poland) together with the Jews from other places who had sought refuge there.
1788	Haidamacks massacre the Jews of Uman (Poland):

	20,000 Jews and Poles killed.
1790–92	Destruction of most of the Jewish communities of Morocco.
1791	Pale of Settlements—twenty-five provinces of czarist Russia established, where Jews permitted permanent residence: Jews forbidden to settle elsewhere in Russia.
1805	Massacre of Jews in Algeria.
1819	A series of anti-Jewish riots in Germany that spread to several neighboring countries (Denmark, Poland, Latvia and Bohemia) known as Hep! Hep! riots, from the derogatory rallying cry against the Jews in Germany.
1827	Compulsory military service for the Jews of Russia: Jewish minors under 18 years of age, known as "Cantonists," placed in preparatory military training establishments.
1835	Oppressive constitution for the Jews in Russia issued by Czar Nicholas I.
1840	Blood libel in Damascus (The Damascus Affair).
1853	Blood libel in Saratov (Russia), bringing a renewal of the blood libel throughout Russia.
1858	Abduction of a 7-year-old Jewish child, Edgardo Mortara, in Bologna by Catholic conversionists (Mortara Case), an episode which aroused universal indignation in liberal circles.
1878	Adolf Stoecker, German anti-Semitic preacher and politician, founds the Social Workers' Party, which marks the beginning of the political anti-Semitic movement in Germany.
1879	Heinrich von Treitschke, German historian and politician, justifies the anti-Semitic campaigns in Germany, bringing anti-Semitism into learned circles.
1879	Wilhelm Marr, German agitator, coins the term anti-Semitism.
1881–84	Pogroms sweep southern Russia: beginning of mass Jewish emigration.

1882	Blood libel in Tiszaeszlar, Hungary, which aroused public opinion throughout Europe.
1882	First International Anti-Jewish Congress convened at Dresden, Germany.
1882	A series of "temporary laws" confirmed by Czar Alexander III of Russia in May, 1882 ("May Laws"), which adopted a systematic policy of discrimination with the object of removing the Jews from their economic and public positions.
1885	Expulsion of about 10,000 Russian Jews, refugees of 1881–1884 pogroms, from Germany.
1891	Blood libel in Xanten, Germany.
1891	Expulsion from Moscow, Russia.
1893	Karl Lueger establishes in Vienna the anti-Semitic Christian Social Party and becomes mayor in 1897.
1894	Alfred Dreyfus' trial in Paris.
1895	Alexander C. Cuza organizes the Alliance Anti-sémitique Universelle in Bucharest, Rumania.
1899	Houston Stewart Chamberlain, racist and anti-Semitic author, publishes his *Die Grundlagen des 19 Jahrhunderts*, which became a basis of National-Socialist ideology.
1899	Blood libel in Bohemia (the Hilsner case).
1903	Pogrom at Kishinev, Russia.
1905	Pogroms in the Ukraine and Bessarabia, perpetuated in 64 towns (most serious in Odessa with over 300 dead and thousands wounded).
1905	First Russian public edition of the *Protocols of the Elders of Zion* appears.
1906	Pogroms in Bialystok and Siedlce, Russia.
1909–10	Polish boycott against Jews.
1911–13	Menahem Mendel Beilis, blood libel trial at Kiev.
1912	Pogroms in Fez (Morocco).
1915	Ku Klux Klan, rascist organization in the U.S., refounded.
1917–21	Pogroms in the Ukraine and Poland. 1) Pogroms by retreating Red Army from the Ukraine (spring,

1918), before the German army. 2) Pogroms by the retreating Ukraine army under the command of Simon Petlyura, resulting in the deaths of over 8,000 Jews. 3) Pogroms by the counterrevolutionary "White Army" under the command of General A. I. Denikin (fall, 1919) in which about 1,500 Jews were killed. 4) Pogroms by the "White Army" in Siberia and Mongolia (1919). 5) Pogroms by anti-Soviet bands in the Ukraine (1920–21), in which thousands of Jews were killed.

1919 Abolishment of community organization and non-Communist Jewish institutions in Soviet Russia.

1919 Pogroms in Hungary: c. 3,000 Jews killed.

1920 Adolf Hitler becomes *Fuehrer* of the National-Sozialistische Deutsche Arbeiterpartei (NSDAP), later known as National Socialist.

1920 Henry Ford I begins a series of anti-Semitic articles based on the *Protocols of the Elders of Zion*, in his *Dearborn Independent*.

1924 Economic restrictions on Jews in Poland.

1925–27 Adolf Hitler's *Mein Kampf* appears.

1933 Adolf Hitler appointed chancellor of Germany. Anti-Jewish economic boycott: first concentration camps (Dachau, Oranienburg, Esterwegen and Sachsenburg).

1935 Nuremberg Laws introduced.

1937 Anti-Semitic legislation in Rumania.

1937 Discrimination against Jews in Polish universities.

1938 After *Anschluss*, pogroms in Vienna, anti-Jewish legislation introduced: deportations to camps in Austria and Germany.

1938 Charles E. Coughlin, Roman Catholic priest, starts anti-Semitic weekly radio broadcasts in U.S.

1938 *Kristallnacht*, Nazi anti-Jewish outrage in Germany and Austria (Nov. 9–10, 1938): Jewish businesses attacked, synagogues burnt, Jews sent to concentration camps.

210 1938 Racial legislation introduced in Italy (Nov. 17, 1938).

Anti-Jewish economic legislation in Hungary.

1939   Anti-Jewish laws introduced in the Protectorate (Czechoslovakia).

1939   Outbreak of World War II (Sept. 1, 1939), Poland overrun by German army; pogroms in Poland; beginning of the Holocaust.

1940   Nazi Germany introduces gassing.

1940   Formation of ghettos in Poland; mass shootings of Jews; Auschwitz camp, later an extermination camp, established; Western European Jews under Nazis. Belzec extermination camp established.

1940   Algerian administration applies social laws of Vichy.

1941   Germany invades Russia and the Baltic states. Majdanek extermination camp established. Chelmno and Treblinka extermination camps established. Anti-Jewish laws in Slovakia. Pogroms in Jassy, Rumania. Pogroms and massacres by the *Einsatzgruppen* and native population in Baltic states and the part of Russia occupied by Germany. Expulsions of Jews from the German Reich to Poland. Beginning of deportation and murder of Jews in France.

1941   Severe riots against Jews in Iraq in consequence of Rashid Ali al-Jiliani's *coup d'état*. Nazi Germany introduces gassing in extermination camps.

1942   Conference in Wannsee, Berlin, to carry out the "Final Solution" (Jan. 20, 1942).

Beginning of mass transports of Jews of Belgium and Holland to Auschwitz.

Massacres in occupied Russia continue. Death camps of Auschwitz, Majdanek and Treblinka begin to function at full capacity; transports from ghettos to death camps.

Sobibor extermination camp established.

1943   Germany declared *Judenrein*. Transports of Jews from all over Europe to death camps. Final liquidation of the Warsaw ghetto (May 16, 1943). Annihilation of most of the ghettos. Transport of

	Italian Jews to death camps.
1944	Extermination of Hungarian Jewry.
1945	Germany surrenders (May 8, 1945) estimated Jewish victims in the Holocaust 5,820,960.
1946	Pogroms at Kielce, Poland, 42 Jews murdered and many wounded (July 4, 1946).
1948	Jewish culture in U.S.S.R. suppressed and Jewish intellectuals shot.
1948	Pogroms in Libya.
1952	Prague Trials (Slánský): Murder of Yiddish intellectuals in Russia and many Jews disappear or sent to work camps.
1953	Accusation of "Doctors' plot" in the U.S.S.R., cancelled with Stalin's death.
1956	Jews of Egypt expelled.
1967	Arabic version of the *Protocols of the Elders of Zion* published in Egypt.
1968	Fresh wave of anti-Semitism in Poland; emigration of most of the remaining Jews of Poland.
1969	Jews executed in Iraq.
1970	Leningrad, and other trials of Soviet Jews, who agitate for right to emigrate.

ABBREVIATIONS

AJHSP	*American Jewish Historical Society—Publications* (after vol. 50=AJHSQ)
Baer, Spain	Yitzhak Baer, *A History of the Jews in Christian Spain,* 2 vols. (1961-66)
Baron, Community	S. W. Baron, *The Jewish Community, its History and Structure to the American Revolution,* 3 vols. (1942)
Baron, Social	S. W. Baron, *A Social and Religious History of the Jews,* 3 vols. (1937); enlarged, 1-2(1952²), 3-14(1957-69)
Dubnow, Hist	S. Dubnow, *History of the Jews* (1967)
Dubnow, Hist Russ	S. Dubnow, *History of the Jews in Russia and Poland,* 3 vols. (1916-20)
Dubnow, Weltgesch	S. Dubnow, *Weltgeschichte des juedischen Volkes,* 10 vols. (1925-29)
EJ	*Encyclopaedia Judaica* (German, A-L only), 10 vols. (1928-34)
Elbogen, Century	I. Elbogen, *Century of Jewish Life* (1960²)
HJ	*Historia Judaica* (1938-61)
HUCA	*Hebrew Union College Annual* (1904; 1924ff.)
JA	*Journal asiatique* (1822 ff.)
JE	*Jewish Encyclopaedia,* 12 vols. (1901-06)
JQR	*Jewish Quarterly Review* (1889ff.)
JSOS	*Jewish Social Studies* (1939ff.)
MGWJ	*Monatsschrift fuer Geschichte und Wissenschaft des Judentums* (1851-1939)
PAAJR	*Proceedings of the American Academy for Jewish Research* (1928ff.)
Pauly-Wissowa	A. F. Pauly, *Realencyclopaedie der klassischen Altertumswissenschaft,* ed. by G. Wissowa et al. (1894ff.)

Reinach, Textes	T. Reinach, *Textes d'auteurs Grecs et Romains relatifs au Judaïsme* (1895; repr. 1963)
Roth, Italy	C. Roth, *The History of the Jews of Italy* (1946)
Shunami, Bibl	S. Shunami, *Bibliography of Jewish Bibliographies* (1965²)
YLBI	*Year Book of the Leo Baeck Institute* (1956ff.)

GLOSSARY

Ḥazakah, acquiring ownership or proving ownership or rights in property.

Judenrat, council set up in Jewish communities and ghettos under the Nazis to execute their instructions.

Marrano(s), descendant(s) of Jew(s) in Spain and Portugal whose ancestors had been converted to Christianity under pressure but who secretly observed Jewish rituals.

Maskil (pl. maskilim), adherent of Haskalah ("Enlightenment") movement.

Maẓẓah (pl. Maẓẓot), unleavened bread.

Mellah, Jewish quarter in North African towns.

Minyan, group of ten male adult Jews, the minimum required for communal prayer.

Shammash, synagogue beadle.

S.S., Nazi formation established in 1925 which later became the "elite" organization of the Nazi party and carried out central tasks in the "Final Solution."

Yishuv, the Jewish community in Ereẓ Israel in the pre-State period.

BIBLIOGRAPHY

Antiquity: Reinach, Textes; H. J. B. Anatole Leroy-Beaulieu, *Israel Among the Nations* (1895); M. Radin, *Jews among Greeks and Romans* (1915); H. I. Bell, *Jews and Christians in Egypt* (1924); Pauly-Wissowa, Suppl. 5 (1931); J. W. Parkes, *The Conflict of the Church and the Synagogue: A Study in the Origins of Antisemitism* (1969); idem, *Antisemitism, A New Analysis* (1969); M. Simon, *Verus Israel* (1948); A. Tcherikover, *Hellenistic Civilization and the Jews* (1961); J. Isaac, *The Teaching of Contempt: Christian Roots of Anti-Semitism* (1964).

Middle Ages: J. C. Wagenseil (ed.), *Tela ignea Satanae* (Lat., 1681); A. L. Williams, *Adversus Judaeos* (Eng., 1935); J. W. Parkes, *The Jew in the Medieval Community* (1938); C. Roth, in: I. Davidson (ed.), *Essays and Studies . . . Linda R. Miller* (1938), 171–90; J. Trachtenberg, *The Devil and the Jew* (1943); G. Kisch, *The Jews in Medieval Germany* (1970²); B. Blumenkrantz, *Juifs et Chrétiens dans le monde occidental 430–1096* (1960).

Modern Times: B. Lazare, *Anti-Semitism, its History and Causes* (1903); H. Coudenhove-Calergy, *Antisemitism Through the Ages* (1935); H. Valentin, *Antisemitism Historically and Critically Examined* (1936); J. Maritain, *A Christian Looks at the Jewish Question* (1939); J. Graeber and S. H. Britt (editors), *Jews in a Gentile World* (1942); K. S. Pinson (ed.), *Essays on Antisemitism* (1946²); M. Hay, *The Foot of Pride: the Pressure of Christendom on the People of Israel for 1900 Years* (1950); N. W. Ackerman and M. Jahoda, *Anti-Semitism and Emotional Disorder, A Psychological Interpretation* (1950); P. F. Bernstein, *Jew-Hate as a Sociological Problem* (1951); R. Loewenstein, *Christians and Jews: a Psychoanalytic Study* (1951, 1963); G. W. Allport, *Nature of Prejudice* (1954); F. Lovsky, *Anti-sémitisme et mystére d'Israël* (1955); L. Poliakov, *Harvest of Hate* (1954); idem, *Histoire de l'antisémitisme*, 3 vols. (1955–68, *History of Antisemitism*, vol. 1, 1965); G. Langmuir, *From Xenophobia to Prejudice* (1957); J. H. E. Fried, in: *Yad Vashem Studies*, 3 (1959),

17–24; A. Bein, *ibid.,* 7–15; idem, *The Jewish Parasite* . . . (1964, offprint from YLBI, vol. 9); idem, *The Jewish Question in Modern Anti-Semitic Literature* . . . (offprint from *In the Dispersion,* 4 (Winter 1964/65), 126–54); idem, in: *Between East and West: Essays* . . . *Bela Horovitz* (1958), 164–93; P. G. J. Pulzer, *Rise of Political Anti-Semitism in Germany and Austria* (1964); E. H. Flannery, *Anguish of the Jews* (1965); J. P. Sartre, *Antisemite and Jew* (1965); Ch. Y. Glock and R. Stark, *Christian Belief and Antisemitism* (1966); M. Meyer, in: YLBI, 11 (1966), 137–70; N. Cohn, *Warrant for Genocide* (1967); S. Esh, in: *Yad Vashem Studies,* 6 (1967), 83–120; A. Hertzberg, *The French Enlightenment and the Jew* (1968); U. Tal, *Yahadut ve-Nazrut ba-Reich ha-Sheni* (1969); American Jewish Committee, *Selected Bibliography of Anti-Semitism* (1942); E. Reichman, *Hostages of Civilization* (1950); G. Mosse, *The Crisis of German Ideology* (1964); P. Massing, *Rehearsal for Destruction* (1949); D. Strong, *Organized Antisemitism in America* (1941); R. Byrnes, *Antisemitism in Modern France* (1950); H. Arendt, *The Origins of Totalitarianism* (1958[2]); J. Higham, in: *AJHSP,* 47 (1957–58), 1–33; J. Lendvai, *Anti-Semitism in Eastern Europe* (1972).

Arab Anti-Semitism: S. G. Haim, in: JSOS, 17 (1952), 307–12; idem, *Arab Nationalism, an Anthology* (1962); Y. Harkabi, *Bein Yisrael le-Arav* (1968); idem, *Emdat ha-Aravim be-Sikhsukh Yisrael Arav* (1968).

In the U.S.S.R.: Jewish Library, London, *Yevrei i Yevreyskiy Narod* (1960–), photostat of material from Soviet daily and periodical press; R. L. Braham, *Jews in the Communist World: A Bibliography 1945–1960* (1961); P. Meyer et al., *Jews in the Soviet Satellites* (1953); S. M. Schwarz, *Jews in the Soviet Union* (1951); idem, *Anti-Semitism in the Soviet Union* (1952); idem, *Yevrei v Sovetskom Soyuze* (1966); *Jews in Eastern Europe,* a periodical survey of events affecting Jews in the Soviet bloc (1958–); B. Z. Goldberg, *Jewish Problem in the Soviet Union* (1961); S. W. Baron, *The Russian Jew under Tsars and Soviets* (1964); J. Gilboa, *The Black Years of Soviet Jewry* (1972).

Blood Libel: M. Samuel, *Blood Accusation* (1966); M. Hacohen (ed.) *Mishpatim ve-Alilot Dam* (1967); H. L. Strack, *The Jew and Human Sacrifice* (1909); C. Roth, *Ritual Murder Libel and the Jew* (1935); D. Hruby, in: W. P. Eckert and E. L. Ehrlich (eds.), *Judenhass-Schuld der Christen?* (1964), 281–308; idem, in: *Der Judenchrist* (1960/62); J. Trachtenberg, *Devil and the Jews* (1943), 124–55; Baer, Spain, 2 (1966), 398–423; *Il Piccolo martire S.*

Domenichino de Val, Patrono di Chierichetti (1960); M. I. Seiden, *Paradox of Hate* (1967). IN RUSSIA: Dubnow, Hist, s.v., *Ritual Murder Libel;* A. D. Margolin, *Jews of Eastern Europe* (1926), 155–247; A. M. Tager, *Decay of Czarism, The Beiliss Trial* (1935).

Jewish Badge: G. Rezasco, *Segno degli ebrei* (1889); U. Robert, *Signes d'Infamie* ... (1891); F. Singermann, *Kennzeichnung der Juden im Mittelalter* (1915); Kisch, in: HJ, 19 (1957), 89ff.; Lichtenstadter, *ibid.,* 5 (1943), 35ff.; Strauss, in: JSOS, 4 (1942), 59; A. Cohen, *Anglo-Jewish Scrapbook* (1943), 249–59; Aronstein, in: *Zion,* 13–14 (1948–49), 33ff.; B. Blumenkranz, *Le Juif médiéval au miroir de l'art chrétien* (1966); S. Grayzel, *Church and the Jews in the XIIIth Century* (1966), index; Baron, Social², 11 (1967), 96–106; A. Rubens, *History of Jewish Costume* (1967), index. NAZI PERIOD: L. Poliakov, *L'Etoile jaune* (1949); G. Reitlinger, *The Final Solution* (1968²), index s.v. *Judenstern.*

Desecration of the Host: A. Ackermann, in: MGWJ, 49(1905), 167–82; J. Miret y Sans, in: *Anuari de l'Institut d'Estudis Catalans,* 4 (1911–12); P. Browe, in: *Roemische Quartalschrift fuer christliche Alterthumskunde,* 34 (1926), 167–97; P. Lefevre, in: *Revue d'Histoire ecclésiastique,* 28 (1932), 329–46; J. Trachtenberg, *The Devil and the Jews* (1943), index; C. Roth, *Personalities and Events in Jewish History* (1953), 60–62; Baer, Spain, 2 (1961), 38–39, 88–90.

Wandering Jew: J. Gaer, *Legend of the Wandering Jew* (1961); G. K. Anderson, *Legend of the Wandering Jew* (1965); Baron, Social², 11 (1967), 177–82; J. Karlowicz, in: *Biblioteka Warszawska,* 3 (1900), 1–13; 214–32; F. Rosenberg, *From Shylock to Svengali* (1960); L. Neubauer, *Die Sage vom ewigen Juden* (1893); A. Yarmolinsky, in: *Studies in Jewish Bibliography and Related Subjects* (1929; Slavic treatments of legend); A. Scheiber, in: *Midwest Folklore,* 4 (1954), 221–35; 6 (1956), 155–8 (Hungarian treatments); F. Kynass, *Der Jude im deutschen Volkslied* (1934); H. C. Holdschmidt, *Der Jude auf dem Theater des deutschen Mittelalters* (1935).

The Ghetto: D. Philipson, *Old European Jewries* (1894), L. Wirth, *The Ghetto* (1928; repr. 1956); A. Pinthus, *Die Judensiedlungen der deutschen Staedte* (1931); I. Abrahams, *Jewish Life in the Middle Ages* (1932²), index, s.v. *Ghetto;* R. Giacomelli, in: *Archivum romanicum,* 16 (1932), 556–63; 17 (1933), 415–44; Roth, Italy, index; idem, in: *Romania,* 60 (1934), 67–74; J. R. Marcus, *Jew in the Medieval World* (1938), index, s.v. *Ghetto;* R.

Anchel, in: JSOS, 2 (1940), 45–60; Baron, Community, index, s.v.

Quarters, Jewish; Baron, Social², index, s.v. *Ghetto;* 9 (1965), 32–36; 11(1967), 87–96; I. Cohen, *Travels in Jewry* (1952), index, s.v. *Ghetto.* JEWISH QUARTERS IN MUSLIM COUNTRIES: H. Z. Hirschberg, in: *Eretz-Israel,* 4 (1956), 226–30; idem, in: A. J. Arberry (ed.), *Religion in the Middle East,* 1 (1969), 130, 154–5; R. Brunschvig, *Berbérie orientale sous les Ḥafṣides,* 1 (1940), 415–6; M. Gaudefroy-Demombynes, in: JA, 2 (1914), 651–8; S. D. Goitein, *Jews and Arabs* (1964), 74–75 and passim.

Expulsions: S. P. Rabinowitz, *Moza'ei Golah* (1894); B. L. Abrahams, in: JQR, 7 (1894/95), 75–100, 236–58, 428–58; A. Marx, *ibid.,* 20 (1907/08), 240–71; R. Straus, *Die Judengemeinde Regensburg im ausgehenden Mittelalter* (1932); idem (ed.), *Urkunden und Aktenstuecke zur Geschichte der Juden in Regensburg* (1960); E. M. Kulisher, *Europe on the Move* (1948), index, s.v. *Jews;* I. Sonne, *Mi-Paulo ha-Revi'i ad Pi'us ha-Ḥamishi* (1954); Baer, Spain, index; JSOS, index.

Pogroms: Zionist Organization, *Die Judenpogrome in Russland,* 2 vols. (1909); Dubnow, Hist Russ, 3 (1920), index; Yevreyskoye istoriko-etnograficheskoye obshchestvo, *Materialy dlya istorii anti-yevreyskikh pogromov v Rossii,* 2 vols. (1919–23); I. Halpern, *Sefer ha-Gevurah,* 2 (1944), 104–58; 3 (1951), 1–229; E. Heifetz, *The Slaughter of the Jews in the Ukraine in 1919* (1921); Committee of Jewish Delegations, *The Pogroms in the Ukraine* (1927); L. Khazanovich, *Der Idisher Khurbn in Ukraine* (1920); E. Tcherikower, *Antisemitizm un Pogromen in Ukraine 1917–1918* (1923); idem, *Di Ukrainer Pogromen in Yor 1919* (1965); J. Schechtman, *Pogromy dobrovolcheskoy armii na Ukraine* (1932); N. Gergel, *Di Pogromen in Ukraine* (1928); A. D. Rosenthal, *Megillat ha-Tevaḥ,* 3 vols. (1927–31); A. Druyanow (ed.), *Reshumot,* 3 (1923); R. Feigenberg, *A Pinkas fun a Toyter Shtot* (1926); *Yevreyskiye pogromy 1918–1921—album* (1926); He-Avar, 9 (1962), 3–81; 10 (1963), 5–149; 17 (1970), 3–136.

Protocols of the Elders of Zion: N. Cohn, *Warrant for Genocide* (1967), a bibliographical note dealing with numerous earlier works can be found in this work; L. Poliakov, *Histoire de l'antisémitisme,* 3 vols. (1955–68), passim; Y. Harkabi, *Arab Attitudes to Israel* (1971).

Anti-Semitic Political Parties and Organizations: S. W. Baron, *The Russian Jew Under Tsars and Soviets* (1964); H. Bender, *Der Kampf um die Judenemanzipation in Deutschland . . .* (1939); R. F. Byrnes, *Antisemitism in Modern France* (1950); N. Cohn, *Warrant for Genocide* (1967); Dubnow, Hist Russ, 2 (1918), 3

(1920), index; J. Frumkin and G. Aronson (eds.), *Russian Jewry 1860–1917* (1966); L. Greenberg, *Jews in Russia,* index; Mahler, in: K. Pinson (ed.), *Essays on Antisemitism* (1946²), 145–73; Vishniak, *ibid.,* 121–45; P. W. Massing, *Rehearsal for Destruction* (1949); P. G. J. Pulzer, *Rise of Political Antisemitism in Germany and Austria* (1964); I. Schapira, *Der Antisemitismus in der franzoesischen Literatur* (1927); K. Schickert, *Die Judenfrage in Ungarn* (1937); E. Sterling, *Er ist wie Du* (1956); Stern-Taeubler, in: HUCA, 23 (1950/51), 171–97; V. Eichstaedt, *Bibliographie zur Geschichte der Judenfrage,* 2 (1938, no more published); E. Silberner, *Ha-Soẓializm ha-Ma'aravi u-She'elat ha-Yehudim* (1955); J. Toury, *Mehumah u-Mevukhah be-Mahpekhat 1848* (1968); U. Tal, *Yahadut ve-Naẓrut ba-Reich ha-Sheni* (1969); Y. Katz, *Bonim Ḥofshiim vi-Yhudim* (1968); N. Katzburg, *Ha-Anti-shemiyyut ha-Politit be-Hungaryah* (dissert., Jerusalem, 1962); N. Rotenstreich, *Ha-Yahadut u-Zekhuyyot ha-Yehudim* (1959); Z. Szajkowski, *Antisemitizm in der Frantsoizisher Arbeter Bavegung* (1948).

Anti-Jewish Boycotts: JE, s.v. *Antisemitism;* EJ, s.v. *Antisemitismus;* Dubnow, Weltgesch, 10˙(1929), 121 and passim; I. Schipper (ed.), *Dzieje handlu żydowskiego na ziemiach polskich* (1937); Elbogen, Century, 639–44; H. G. Reissner, in: *Jubilee Volume . . . Curt C. Silberman* (1969).

Numerus Clausus: CZARIST RUSSIA: Dubnow, Hist Russ, index L. Greenberg, *Jews in Russia: Struggle for Emancipation* (1965); S. Baron, *The Russian Jew under Tsars and Soviets* (1964); J. Kreppel, *Juden und Judentum von heute* (1925), para. 77, 501–4. SOVIET UNION: W. Korey, in: L. Kochan (ed.), *The Jews in Soviet Russia since 1917* (1972²), 90, 94–95; A. Nove and J. A. Newth, *ibid.,* 145, 154–6. POLAND: S. Langnas, *Żydzi a studja akademickie w Polsce* (1933); M. Mirkin, in: *Yidishe Ekonomik,* 2 (1938), 272–6; *Polscki Rocznik statystyczny* (1921–38). HUNGARY: N. Katzburg, in: *Sefer ha-Shanah shel Universitat Bar Ilan,* 4–5 (1956–65), 270–88 (with an English summary); *The Jewish Minority in Hungary. Report by the Secretary and Special Delegate of the Joint Foreign Committee . . .* (1926). UNITED STATES: AJYB, passim; O. and M. F. Handlin, in: AJYB (1955), 75–77.

Discrimination: E. Goldhagen (ed.), *Ethnic Minorities in the Soviet Union* (1968); S. Schwarz, *Jews in the Soviet Union* (1951); W. Korey, in: *Midstream,* 12 no. 5 (1966), 49–61; A. D. Sakharov, *Progress, Coexistence and Intellectual Freedom* (1968); AJYB, 69 (1968); N. C. Belth (ed.), *Barriers: Patterns of Discrimination against Jews*

(1958); B. R. Epstein and A. Forster, *Some of My Best Friends* (1962); *Rights*, 7 no. 1 (Feb., 1968); B'nai B'rith International Council, *Survey, Report 64–1* (Jan., 1964); R. M. Powell, *The Social Milieu as a Force in Executive Promotion* (1969); M. Decter, in: *Foreign Affairs*, 41 (1963), 420–30; B. Z. Goldberg, *Jewish Problem in the Soviet Union* (1961); N. DeWitt, *Education and Professional Employment in the U.S.S.R.* (1961); idem, *The Status of Jews in Soviet Education* (1964).

Theory of Race: M. F. Ashley Montagu, *Man's Most Dangerous Myth: The Fallacy of Race* (1942); H. Kohn, *Idea of Nationalism* (1944); G. W. Allport, *Nature of Prejudice* (1954); UNESCO, *Race Question in Modern Science* (1957); L. L. Snyder, *Idea of Racialism* (1962); L. Poliakov, *Histoire de l'Antisémitisme de Voltaire à Wagner* (1968); S. Conn and E. E. Hunt, *Living Race of Man* (1965); idem, *The Origin of Races* (1962); idem, *The Races of Europe* (1939); idem, *The Story of Man* (1962²); A. R. Jensen, in: *Harvard Educational Review*, 39, no. 1 (Winter 1969), 1–123; 39, no. 2 (Spring 1969), 273–356; L. Edson, in: *The New York Times Magazine* (August 31, 1969), 10–11; M. Deutsch, in: *Harvard Educational Review*, 39, no. 3 (Summer 1969), 523–57.

Neo-Fascism: D. Eisenberg, *The Re-emergence of Fascism* (1967).

The Dreyfus Affair: Shunami, Bibl, 268–9; J. Reinach, *Histoire de l'affaire Dreyfus*, 7 vols. (1901–11); *Le procès Dreyfus . . .*, 3 vols. (1900); *La revision du procès de Rennes*, 3 vols. (1908); P. Dreyfus (ed.), *Dreyfus: His Life and Letters* (1937); Tcher-ski, in: E. Tcherikower (ed.), *Yidn in Frankraykh*, 2 (1942), 155–92 (Eng. abstract: 332); J. Kayser, *The Dreyfus Affair* (1931); R. F. Byrnes, *Antisemitism in Modern France*, 1 (1950); G. Chapman, *The Dreyfus Case: A Reassessment* (1955); N. Halasz, *Captain Dreyfus: The Story of a Mass Hysteria* (1957²); M. Baumont, *Aux sources de l'affaire* (1959); P. Boussel, *L'Affaire Dreyfus et la presse* (1960); L. Derfler (ed.), *Dreyfus Affair: Tragedy of Errors?* (1963); D. Johnson, *France and the Dreyfus Affair* (1967); B. Schechter, *The Dreyfus Affair: A National Scandal* (1965); M. Paléologue, *My Secret Diary of the Dreyfus Case* (1957); L. Blum, *Souvenirs sur l'Affaire* (1935); M. Marrus, *The Politics of Assimilation* (1971); H. Dardenne, *Lumière sur l'affaire Dreyfus* (1964).

The Beilis Trial: M. Samuel, *Blood Accusation: the Strange History of the Beiliss Case* (1966); M. Beilis, *Story of My Sufferings* (1926); AJYB, 16 (1914/15), 19–89; A. D. Margolin, in: *Jews of Eastern Europe* (1926), 155–247; A. B. Tager, *The Decay of Czarism: The Beiliss Trial* (1935); Z. Szajkowski, in: PAAJR, 31 (1963), 197–218. **221**

The Slánský Trial: R. L. Braham, *Jews in the Communist World: A Bibliography* (1961), 20–22; American Zionist Council, *Public Opinion on the Prague Trial* (1953); K. Kaplan, *Thoughts About The Political Trials* (1968); M. Oren, *Reshimot Asir Prag* (1958); S. Orenstein, *Alilah be-Prag* (1968); idem, *Lefi Pekuddah mi-Moskva* (1969); E. Loebl, *Die Revolution rehabilitiert ihre Kinder* (1968); idem, *Sentenced and Tried* (1969); *Proces s vedením protistátního spikleneckého centra v čele s Rudolfem Slánským* (1953); A. London, *The Confession* (1970); J. Slánská, *Report on My Husband* (1969).

The "Doctors' Plot": R. Conquest, *Power and Policy in the USSR* (1962), index; B. Nicolaevsky, *Power and the Soviet Elite* (1965), passim; S. Schwarz, *Yevreyi v Sovetskom Soyuze s nachala vtoroy mirovoy voyny (1939–65)* (1966), passim.

INDEX

225